The *Art* of
Lionel Trains

Toy Trains and American Dreams

ROGER CARP

KALMBACH
BOOKS

Printed in Canada

03 04 05 06 07 08 09 10 11 12   10 9 8 7 6 5 4 3 2 1

Publisher's Cataloging-in-Publication
(Provided by Quality Books, Inc.)
Carp, Roger.
    The art of Lionel trains : toy trains and American
dreams / Roger Carp.
    p. cm.
    ISBN 0-87116-202-4

    1. Lionel Corporation. 2. Advertising—Railroads—
Models. I. Title.

TF197.C273 2003   625.1'9
                          QBI03-200505

Art Director: Kristi Ludwig

contents

acknowledgments

The generosity and encouragement given to me by so many individuals matched the beauty and grace evident in so many examples of Lionel artwork. Their assistance and support enabled me to conduct the research necessary to write this book. I'm delighted to thank them here.

My good friend Dick Christianson has enabled me for more than a decade to explore the history of Lionel. He suggested that I look at its art, responded enthusiastically as I described my discoveries, and then offered judicious criticism of this manuscript that has improved it.

Ron Antonelli, another close friend, has helped by bringing notable illustrations to my attention, reading every word of my manuscript, and challenging me to deepen my analysis. Whatever merit this book has is due, to a significant degree, to Ron's efforts.

A number of people deserve thanks for letting me examine and photograph the catalogs, magazines, newspapers, brochures, and comic books they own. Two in particular deserve special thanks. Ray Fetzner and John Wickland went out of their way to share dozens of pieces of Lionel art. Without their help I could not have filled this book with so many striking images.

I want as well to thank these hobbyists for their keen eyes and generous spirits: Joe Algozzini, Jim Berilla, Alan Bloore, Jim Burke, Ed Daugherty, Richard Hofmeister, Jeff Lampert, Tom McComas, the late William Mekalian, Ron Morris, Bob Osterhoff, Joe Palermo, Ed Prendeville, the late Lou Redman, Don Simonini, William Sivley, Bruce Stiny, and Greg Stout.

For other favors I am grateful to staff members of Illustration House, the Toy Train Reference Library, and the Train Station of Mountain Lakes, New Jersey. Bruce Manson, editor of the *Train Collectors Quarterly*, has, by publishing overviews of Lionel's advertising and promotional pieces, introduced me to many key images.

I have benefited from the writings of leading scholars in the fields of American art and culture, advertising, railroading, and the history of toys and Lionel trains. They include Gary Cross, Peter Filene, John Gruber, John Kasson, Roland Marchand, Susan Matt, Walt Reed, John Stilgoe, and Michael Zega. David Dansky and Laura Greene offered insightful criticism of a key chapter.

I take great pleasure in being able to express my gratitude to many former Lionel employees. Their memories and insights have raised the level of my understanding of this great toy train maker, its leaders and heritage, and its links to American dreams. My thoughts turn first to these gentlemen, who died before this book appeared: William Bonanno, Jack Kindler, Louis Melchionne, Frank Pettit, and Robert Sherman.

Which catalog illustration or advertisement is your favorite piece of Lionel artwork? Joshua Cowen, the company's founder, might have selected this photograph, taken at the Lionel showroom and run in the *New York Sunday News* of December 4, 1955. It proved that his dreams—of building a successful business and bringing his son, Lawrence, into top management—had come true.

Then I recall others, whose creativity continues to inspire me: Orlando Militano, Roz Relin, Banning Repplier, Cory SerVaas, Bill Vollheim, Arthur Zirul, and Jacques Zuccaire. Among other individuals discussed, especially artists, I wish to thank the families of Joseph Adda, Fernando Ciavatti, Lawrence Cowen, Raymond Crowley, Joseph Hanson, and Wesley Neff (all deceased) for sharing information.

At Kalmbach Publishing Co., I received guidance and encouragement from many colleagues and friends, including Mary Algozin, Neil Besougloff, Jim Forbes, Kent Johnson, Bob Keller, Russ Larson, Kevin Rausch, Jim Riccioli, Terry Thompson, and William Zuback. Candice St. Jacques and Julia Gerlach improved the text with their insightful comments and editing. Kristi Ludwig earns special thanks for laying out the book with great skill. I'm sure that, in a previous life, she designed a Lionel catalog or two.

I appreciate, too, the firm support of current and former executives at Lionel LLC. Among those who helped are William Bracy, John W. Brady, Jim Bunte, Richard Kughn, Julie Laird, Richard Maddox, Charlotte Montgomery, and Todd Wagner.

My greatest debts are owed to my family. My sister, Sue Silbert, taught me how to enjoy the Lionel freight set I received in 1956 and why I should always treasure my toys. My parents, Robert and Bee Gee Carp, gave me that train. As importantly, they encouraged me, decades later, to study Lionel's history and write about it with seriousness and flair. And they nurtured a love of both the fine arts and commercial illustrations such as those described here. My late father taught me to look at paintings and see how their beauty enriches life and makes dreams come true. My sons, Benjamin and Daniel, continue to fill those dreams.

introduction

Lionel remains one of the most recognized brand names in America. Some 50 years after toy trains reached unprecedented heights of popularity, everyone who grew up in the middle of the past century seems to remember the shining lights, puffs of smoke, and smell of ozone associated with those charming toys. Baby boomers recall their trains as wonderful playthings.

What they may not realize is that marketing convinced the public that youngsters needed Lionel trains. The text of advertisements was strong and direct, but the lasting message that Lionel wished to convey came through in art-work. Images of fathers and sons, of boys and locomotive engineers, of lads with their hands on the throttle as they prepared for manhood—these helped Lionel show that a train was essential to a happy and productive childhood.

Browsing through examples of advertising art still brings pleasure. Beyond this enjoyment, though, there are other reasons to study the finest of Lionel's illustrations and photographs. Doing so brings back memories of the trains and accessories that have delighted generations of children. It also draws attention to illustrators

who might otherwise be forgotten. Third, analysis of various examples of artwork sheds light on the different goals set for the company by Lionel's founder and successors right to the present. Finally, it links toys and their depictions with American cultural values and social roles, especially notions of masculinity, by showing how Lionel sought to increase sales by persuad-ing consumers that its trains could answer hopes and relieve anxieties.

sources and illustrators

Following the lead of German and American toy makers, Lionel issued annual catalogs. By the 1920s, what youngsters referred to as Lionel's "wish books" dominated the market and eventually became icons of childhood in America. But even before then, illustrations of Lionel trains appeared in catalogs peddling appliances and hardware, as well as in advertise-ments aimed at the toy trade and the burgeon-ing industry of "electrical novelties."

Other pictures showed up in mass-circulation magazines and publications reaching juvenile audiences, primarily boys. Noteworthy among the illustrations directed at kids were color advertisements in the comics sections of Sunday newspapers. These ads, which first appeared in the early 1920s, were joined in the mid-1930s by similar pitches in comic books.

Posters and placards often enhanced the static and animated displays that Lionel, on its own or in conjunction with advertising agencies, created for retailers. Memorable drawings and photographs surfaced in *Lionel Magazine* and then *Model Builder*, periodicals that the firm launched in the 1930s to showcase its merchandise. They also appeared in pamphlets and books that Lionel put out in the 1940s and '50s to promote its trains and the hobby of model railroading.

A commitment to aesthetics influenced everything associated with Lionel. Evidence ranges from the printing on its orange-and-blue boxes to the modernistic look of its remodeled showrooms in New York and Chicago, from the design of its annual reports to the pins awarded for longtime service and the stylish double-breasted suits worn by the company's salesmen. Even Lionel's stationery featured illustrations. These sources, like the art filling catalogs and magazines, attest to an understanding among leaders that presentation was critical. They rec-

ognized that artistic touches made Lionel stand out and that positive impressions boosted sales.

In the past quarter-century or so, evocative paintings and illustrations have given way to photographs that range from sublime to mundane. Photography began influencing the way Lionel showed its trains and accessories as far back as the 1910s, with great shots distinguishing advertisements and corporate publications from the 1930s on. Brilliant use of lighting combined with thoughtful compositions, creating shots that generated excitement about the trains and nostalgia for a time gone by.

Operating Lionel trains, like caring for a dog, promised to offer a boy unlimited fun while preparing him for the responsibilities of adulthood. He learned about engineering, electronics, and transportation and never lost his smile, as shown on the cover of the 1926 catalog. Walter Beach Humphrey painted this heartwarming scene. Like many examples of Lionel art, the image and message were geared mainly toward boys. Gender-based advertising has dominated the American toy industry for most of its history.

Regardless of the medium used, artists managed, by depicting trains in diverse settings, often under the control of a boy, to show how much fun these toys were. They used dazzling colors and bold poses to make Lionel trains seem large, fast, and exciting. Thanks to their efforts, people became familiar with these playthings and generations of boys came of age wishing for a set and spending countless hours playing with one.

The early history of Lionel coincided with what historians label the golden age of American illustration. They analyze the styles of Howard

Pyle, Charles Dana Gibson, James Montgomery Flagg, and Maxfield Parrish, and they laud breakthroughs in printing and the development of popular magazines driven by eye-catching illustrations. Scholars interested in work done in the middle of the 20th century, a time when Lionel art reached great heights, assess the "sentimental realism" of Norman Rockwell and the politically conscious work of Rockwell Kent, and consider how J.C. Leyendecker and John Held created new standards of fashion for men and women.

Missing from academic accounts are the illustrators responsible for Lionel art. The reason for this omission, one might assume, is obvious. From an artistic perspective, Lionel illustrations fail to measure up to what was achieved by the painters that scholars and collectors are at last acknowledging as masters. In fact, most of Lionel art lacks any attribution. All one can surmise about the unsigned catalog covers and magazine illustrations is that they likely were executed by artists employed by advertising agencies in New York City. These painters turned out the dozens of small, simple catalog renderings that Lionel needed each year. Occasionally, one of the paintings used on the cover of Lionel's annual catalog or for its advertisements was signed. A few of those names—Walter Beach Humphrey, Raymond Thayer, L. Meinrad Mayer, and Alex Ross—elicit nods of recognition from specialists in the field of American commercial illustration.

Other artists, such as Jon O. Brubaker, Wesley Neff, and Fernando E. Ciavatti, are all but forgotten. But the pictures these men executed indicate that they were talented and imaginative. When asked to create illustrations that conveyed the pleasures of a miniature locomotive, passenger set, or station, they—and their unidentified peers—responded with images that satisfied Lionel management at the time and still captivate toy train enthusiasts today.

These artists deserve their place in the sun, although their talents need not be overestimated. Quite frankly, Lionel either could not afford the very best or, more to the point, did not need the very best. Pleasing images of boys and others with toy trains met the company's demands because they were able to gain national recognition without the advertising ploys and artistic gimmicks other firms depended on. Lionel art never featured an icon, such as Mr. Peanut or the Green Giant. No

mascot showed up, except for a brief time in the 1900s and again in the late 1950s, when a lion (obviously) appeared. Unlike most full-sized railroads, Lionel did not ask its artists to design a herald that it could plaster on the side of a tender or boxcar.

Instead, advertising and sales executives let the trains sell themselves. They wanted artwork, whether simple hand-drawn etchings or, more recently, complex computer-generated graphics, merely to improve the already colorful appearance of individual models and sets. Illustrations and photographs had only to make Lionel

Lionel aimed to offer models of the newest trains making headlines. Streamliners caught everyone's attention in the 1930s, and soon O gauge replicas hit the market. This advertisement in the *Chicago Tribune* of November 28, 1937, showcases such classics as the nos. 267E *Flying Yankee* (second from left) and 299W Union Pacific *City of Denver* (fourth from left).

text continues on page 12

a range of sources

The sources of Lionel's art are diverse. Early each year, an advance catalog went to wholesalers and distributors. It occasionally had color covers, along with black-and-white drawings and photographs of what Lionel planned to offer. Magazine ads, especially those in publications aimed at families, featured great illustrations, with some of the finest dating from the prosperous years after the two world wars. Other images appeared in media for kids. Lionel was among the first toy makers to put ads in Sunday supplements and comic books. Vivid colors and exciting views nurtured dreams.

Kids didn't have to live in the Santa Fe's territory to be awed by its red-and-silver diesels and streamlined cars. That's why the no. 2190W Super Speedliner set graced the cover of the advance catalog for 1953.

Above: Lionel reached kids by advertising in comic books between the 1930s and 1950s. Who could skip over this page in the December 1946 *True Comics*, with great locomotives, accessories, and mail-in offers?

Right: Starting in the early 1920s and continuing into the late 1950s, Lionel placed ads in the color supplements of metropolitan newspapers during the holiday season. This one appeared in the *Chicago Herald American* of November 5, 1949.

trains seem more glamorous, entertaining, and thrilling. In achieving this end, art left boys and men believing that an electric train was vital to their happiness and growth.

levels of understanding

With color, animation, and enjoyment bursting forth from every train, depictions of them naturally contain vibrancy and charm. Little wonder that glances at advertising art and catalog photographs bring smiles and revive memories of the joy associated with a train set.

But Lionel's art can be understood on more than one level. Digging deeper shows how illustrative styles changed. Composition, lighting, and perspective rarely stayed constant, as creators looked for better ways of making trains seem irresistible. Showing a model by itself was not enough. Artists enhanced its appeal by exaggerating features and depicting it in a dramatic setting. Sharper colors and crisper details also revealed advances in the ways that illustrations were printed.

Focusing on art executed at different times in the history of Lionel sheds light on corporate goals and the strategies that executives devised for winning over the public. Maximizing sales remained paramount, but the tactics employed to maintain interest in trains changed because children's tastes evolved and popular appreciation of Lionel products waxed and waned. Artists, eager to touch the fantasies and anxieties of consumers, learned that posing children with trains (sometimes inserting adults, too) suggested a nurturing, reassuring relationship between Lionel products and customers. Illustrations thus reinforced the idea that, as executives at Lionel have long contended, this is a business worth trusting because it wants to make its customers happy.

How Lionel brings happiness has changed, a point that's best seen through art. Illustrations make it plain that the company's identity has changed as decision-makers have debated what it is they produce. For example, the images of trains, motors, and batteries seen in early catalogs do not bring to mind a toy maker. Art depicted these products as somewhat sophisticated electrical appliances of interest to the curious and daring. Adults were the intended audience, as they were as likely to display an operating train in a store window as on the floor at home.

Before many years passed, however, illustrations became more fanciful to convey the wish that Lionel's trains be considered toys. That idea proved to be financially sound and emotionally satisfying to the company's founder, Joshua Lionel Cohen (who Anglicized his name to Cowen in 1910), as it has, to varying degrees, to the men who have followed in his footsteps at Lionel. Some of the most colorful illustrations and photographs show the trains as playthings that race and flash. Kids gazed at these pictures, which became the basis of dreams.

Lionel has never abandoned images that emphasize the toy-like qualities of its trains. Still, as early as the 1910s and continuing to the present, art has offered a divergent perspective that supplements and conflicts with the notion that trains are playthings. Lionel has promoted this alternative view to earn the trust of the adults who buy trains for their families and to extend its market by winning over older boys who might spurn trains for more mature and more masculine activities.

Art has forwarded the idea that Lionel produces realistic models that mold the boys playing with them. Its trains and accessories replicate the railroads that helped settle America. Sometimes, illustrations make clear, Lionel insists it can offer whimsy and realism

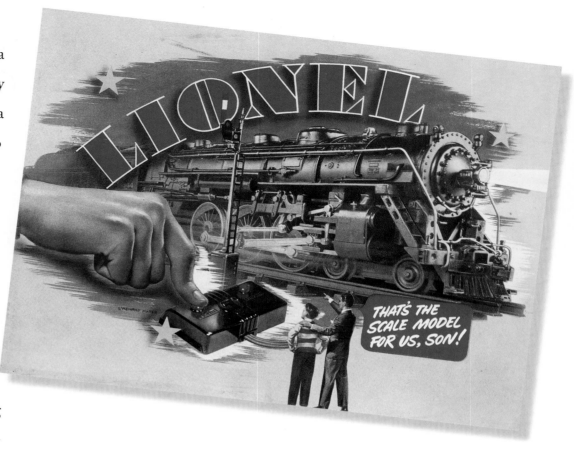

simultaneously, whether by marketing complementary lines or by developing products that feature the best of both worlds.

Illustrations and the words accompanying them underscore the realism of Lionel trains. Models of well-known locomotives and passenger trains appear in contemporary urban, rural, or industrial settings. Freight cars and steam engines take on new identities when shown on tracks running next to a factory or into a metropolitan terminal. Some illustrations pinpoint the mechanical innovations of Lionel locomotives and the superb interior detailing of its

Scale realism, epitomized by the no. 700E Hudson steam locomotive, as well as remote-controlled accessories, represented a new direction in the late pre-World War II era. These developments were perfect for uniting fathers and sons, as shown by L. Meinrad Mayer's cover for the 1940 catalog.

Pullman cars. Others link additions to the line with the latest innovations on actual railroads, from popular streamliners in the 1930s to mammoth diesel-electrics today.

Artists shift their perspective to highlight power and realism. They portray models from the front, so close to the edge of a scene that viewers feel the train will crush them. Upward views and three-quarter angles suggest the mass of locomotives. Techniques that capture the dimensions and details of a boxcar or caboose also leave viewers believing that they are staring at a full-sized piece of equipment.

The trend of illustrators and photographers to underscore the realism of the trains manufactured by Lionel reflects the belief of company executives that this aspect retains its appeal. Kids convinced of the authenticity of their miniature locomotives and cars will not, decision-makers have argued since the 1930s, give them up and switch to other pastimes. To the contrary, children's interest will increase, while adults, who ignore what they perceive as toys, will find themselves attracted to scale models of the most up-to-date trains. Consumers go on buying Lionel products, and their purchases nurture a trusting relationship with the firm. Such loyalty not only guarantees a profitable future for Lionel, it also earns the public's respect for a business seen as protective of families and cherished values.

messages about masculinity

Illustrations also provide insights into the prevailing culture, in particular, the emotional life of the audiences that artists sought to reach. They work in partnership with design engineers and sales personnel to sell electric trains that, like other toys, are expected to instill proper habits and reinforce prevailing social roles in children. Regardless of how frivolous a toy may seem, mothers and fathers demand that it in some way prepare their offspring for adulthood. Analysis of the ways artists depict Lionel trains reveals much about popular values in 20th-century America.

Underlying the firm's campaigns to dominate the market, while appearing to be more than just a toy maker, were issues of masculinity. A theme, perhaps the central one, of Lionel art from the 1920s into the '60s was that owning a train helped a rambunctious boy mature into a well-behaved young man able to assume a place in the world of business. Transformed by his Lionel train, he became the perfect companion for his father, who also changed for the better by operating a set.

Popular thinking held that for a man to be judged successful he had to seize control of his destiny from commercial and social forces conspiring to weaken him. He had to act rationally, exhibit self-reliance and productivity, and cooperate with others. All the while, he had to be on his guard lest his peers erode his initiative. The road a strong, independent man had to walk was strewn with obstacles, but with the right preparation he could thrive in this dangerous environment.

An electric train was, art made plain, essential to the development of a successful man. Illustrations combined with copy to coax parents into buying sets as a means of guiding their sons into an uncertain future. Trains and accessories introduced boys to modern systems of commerce and manufacturing. Lads learned about contemporary transportation and appreciated the heroism of locomotive engineers. The wonders of electricity became familiar, and youngsters grew confident that they, like the young Joshua Cohen, could capitalize on this marvelous source of power.

Other important lessons took hold indirectly. Boys learned how to plan ahead, whether by saving money for more track or by avoiding

One of the Best Ways
Men get to know Each Other

How well do you know your boy? Does he really know you? He's growing fast. Is he growing away from you? Shed those years, drop that dignity, forget those problems. Come down out of the clouds and get down on the floor with your boy and Lionel Trains this Christmas. It will make him happier and you a lot younger. Lionel Trains bring a man and boy closer than anything in the world. See your dealer for the 1950 catalog or send coupon for special offer.

start this Christmas
with LIONEL TRAINS

Now with *MAGNE-TRACTION!*
Lionel's track-gripping triumph that makes trains take amazing grades and curves. *Plus* realistic built-in whistle, smoke, remote-control couplers. And priced lower than in many years past.

collisions when running two trains at once. Thrift, resourcefulness, and other prized habits took root the longer boys kept their trains. Controlling a miniature passenger express or log loader today was sure to inculcate in young men the traits and knowledge they would eventually need to manage an office, ship

The hope that a Lionel set would break down the barriers between sons and fathers comes through in this advertisement in the November 1950 *National Geographic*. Closely knit families promised security in an uncertain world after World War II.

text continues on page 18

The painting done by Fernando E. Ciavatti for the cover of the 1930 catalog uses the conventions of the movement known as Art Deco to capture the beauty and sophistication of the Standard gauge line. Ciavatti worked in New Jersey, where his portraits were hung in a number of churches.

16

style and greatness

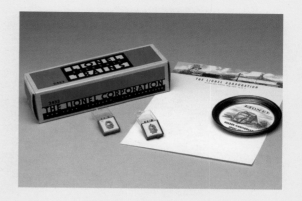

Elegance and grace characterized Lionel because Joshua Cowen aspired to greatness. He dreamed of being more than a toy mogul; he wanted to be counted among the elite of Manhattan. So he Anglicized his surname, wore tailored suits, attended the opera, and voted Republican. Cowen made sure that his firm ("Lionel" hinted at England and aristocracy) reflected his hopes and vision. Great care went into the planning, illustration, and printing of its annual catalogs. The fact that Lionel put out so extensive a catalog every year elevated it above its rivals in the toy field. More evidence of Cowen's wish to exude style and urbanity appears in the typefaces on Lionel's boxes and stationery. Even mundane objects, such as commemorative desk ornaments and employee service pins, serve as evidence of his commitment to excellence and fascination with modernism.

Joshua Cowen wanted everything associated with his firm to be attractive and elegant. Lionel boxes and letterhead, the special coaster created for the company's golden anniversary in 1950, and employee service pins met his high expectations.

things will benefit their children while enriching (or at least not worsening) their own lives.

Executives concluded that the sales of trains would increase as consumers saw these playthings as instruments for shaping boys into hardworking, self-sufficient men, particularly when nervousness about the future was on the upswing. The leaders of Lionel also hoped that young men, inclined on reaching adolescence to leave their trains behind and pursue organized athletics, Scouting, or other "manly" activities, might remain interested if they believed those models were accurate replicas and not just toys.

From a cultural perspective, then, the images shown here have merit, even if they fail to measure up as high art. Studying these illustrations and photographs and relating them to contemporary values, roles, hopes, and fears prove instructive about popular expectations of toys and their meaning for boys and parents. It is on this level, rather than on an aesthetic one, that Lionel artwork assumes significance and deserves to be remembered.

always dreams

Whether yesterday's kids benefited from owning Lionel trains cannot really be measured. Not many grew up to be locomotive engineers

Lionel's corporate philosophy changed after World War II. As the cover that Raymond Crowley painted for its annual report for 1954 reveals, Lionel sought to portray its trains as ideal for families and to diversify its line by entering other hobbies, such as fishing.

cargo, or produce high-quality consumer goods.

That Lionel art linked trains with prevailing roles and values makes sense. Since adults buy most toys, they want the items they select to conform to their beliefs and help them pass those beliefs to their offspring. They need to feel good about their purchases and trust that play-

or accountants at Penn Central or Amtrak. Precious few bought stock in CSX or Norfolk Southern. But those trains left their mark.

Saying "Lionel" to anyone over the age of 40 brings forth nods of recognition and stories of smoking, whistling trains chugging around Christmas trees. Thousands of middle-aged baby boomers have rekindled their love affair with Lionel trains by collecting vintage models and constructing layouts. Many have done so with fervent memories of learning about the pleasures of Lionel from their fathers. Now they seek to revive the past and show their children or grandchildren that a train can bring joy.

It can nurture dreams, too. Lionel art expresses those dreams in two dimensions. Kids dream of having fun and being happy among friends. They dream of learning about the world and striding forward to conquer it. They dream of growing up to be competent and independent, like their fathers, who in turn dream that they will never grow old or lose touch with their kids. Illustrations assure both generations that their dreams can come true as long as they own a Lionel train.

More than a century after the founding of Lionel, its trains continue to improve in every way. The electronically sophisticated, scale-detailed locomotives on the cover of the Winter 2002 issue of *Inside Track*, a company publication, prove that today's toy train enthusiasts are living in a golden age.

chapter one
Dreams of ambition
1900-1923

Dreams have infused Lionel art since black-and-white illustrations filled the first catalogs more than a century ago. Those early dreams belonged to the firm's founder. Joshua Lionel Cohen latched onto miniature electric trains as a way to make his mark in a bustling, open America. Like Louis B. Mayer and Irving Berlin, he was an ambitious "outsider" who created a beloved product that validated and reinforced prevailing values and sentiments. However, during the first two decades of the 20th century, the illustrations in Lionel catalogs and advertisements primarily reflected Cohen's dreams—of who he wanted to be and what his business might become.

Born in 1877, Cohen dreamed yet never let his head drift into the clouds. He preferred to get his hands dirty experimenting rather than keep them clean holding a book. No wonder this son of immigrants dropped out of two colleges in his native New York City to join the ranks of would-be Edisons. While barely out of adolescence, Cohen hitched his wagon to electricity and soon tasted success, patenting a device that set off a photographer's flash powder. That invention, which relied on dry-cell batteries to heat a wire fuse, led to a contract to build bomb fuses for the Navy.

Brimming with confidence after that job, Cohen established a business in September of 1900. Riches and renown had yet to arrive—why, he didn't even have another viable product to sell—but he pushed ahead, desperate for inspiration. In 1901, the story goes, Cohen noticed that pedestrians rarely paused to admire the wares in shop windows in Manhattan. His muse told him to install wheels on a wood box that might have held cheese or cigars. Next, Cohen added a motor that picked up energy

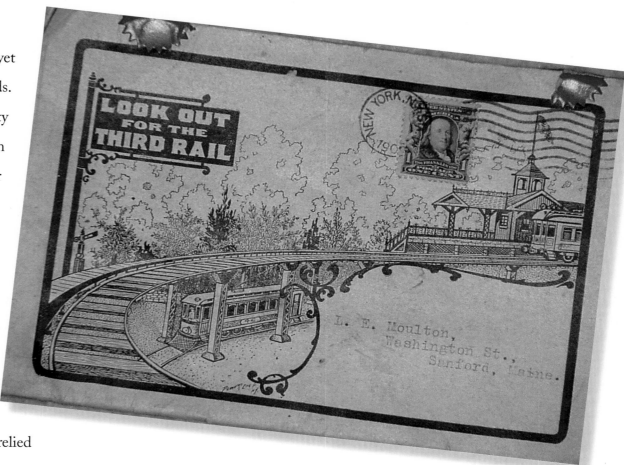

from a dry-cell battery wired to a ring of metal track. One merchant put the arrangement in his storefront and placed an item in the gondola. As Cohen predicted, crowds gathered to watch the sight and then, sufficiently amused, trooped inside to make purchases.

With this display, Cohen joined the ranks of men and businesses making what a century ago were known as "electrical novelties." They played upon the public's fascination with electricity, especially its magical ability to spark movement in inanimate objects. Inventors developed

The cover of the 1906 Lionel catalog brims over with excitement, thanks to the expansion of the product line with trolleys in a new gauge soon to be called "Standard." The warning to "Look Out for the Third Rail" interrupts the quaint charm of this scene.

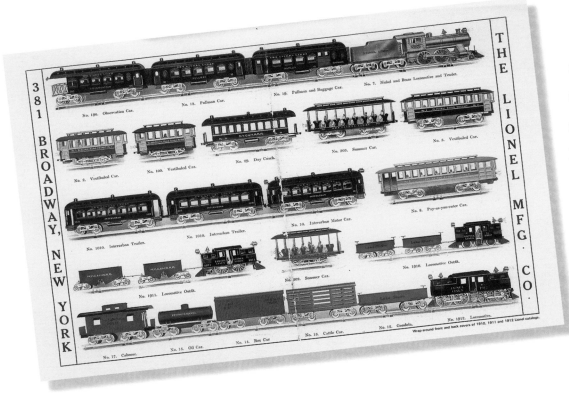

Trolleys, steam locomotives, and a big electric-profile engine highlighted the Standard gauge line, as seen in the wraparound front and back covers of the 1910 Lionel catalog. For the first time, Joshua Cohen paraded his finest trains in full color.

conveniences that saved time, redirected energy, or entertained. Like P.T. Barnum, Cohen was a showman, exploiting people's desire to be amazed and amused. If displays using electricity drew people into shops, so much the better for both the proprietors and their customers.

Quickly, however, consumers demanded more. They wanted their own versions of Cohen's marvel to operate at home. Watching seemed too passive; people wanted to own this electrical novelty. With that, Cohen began envisioning himself as a maker not only of business displays but also of small railroads to delight children and their parents.

He wasn't the first to offer a miniature train, not even the first to sell one powered by electricity. Toy trains emerged almost as soon as full-sized ones did in the early 19th century. Made of wood, tinplated steel, or cast iron, they were pulled by strings or pushed by hand. European and American firms later added motors driven by steam and fueled by alcohol. In time, wet-cell and dry-cell batteries were used, followed by household current diverted to metal tracks.

Locomotives, freight and passenger cars, track, and more swelled the lines sold by such German toy makers as Märklin, Bing, Ernst Planck, and Georges Carrette. By the end of the 19th century, they had added stations, signals, lights, and other accessories. The assortment of decorated items seemed unending as firms strove to provide children with complete systems so they could assemble replicas of the railroads they saw in cities across the Continent.

To show consumers their wares, toy makers, led by Märklin and Bing, printed illustrated catalogs. Boys and girls were encouraged to leaf through these glorified sales brochures to see how much was available before pleading with Mama and Papa to buy it for them. The ploy was simple yet brilliant and, to judge from the growing number of pages in the catalogs, effective.

American rivals, impressed by the success of German firms, imitated them in hopes of overtaking them. Carlisle & Finch, a Cincinnati-based company making electrical items for the home and military, introduced an electric toy train in 1896. Other businesses offered models "powered" by a child's hand and imagination. Leading the way, however, was the Ives Manufacturing Corp. of Bridgeport, Connecticut. Specializing in playthings, it had been selling tinplated locomotives and decorated wood cars since the 1870s. Starting with floor toys, it graduated to models equipped with windup motors like those used in clocks. In 1901, Ives improved its "clockwork" trains so that they operated over standardized track with rails spaced 1¼ inches apart.

Edward and Harry Ives, the father and son who ran Ives, also learned the importance of catalogs from the Germans. They were issuing their own catalogs by the early 1900s, with pictures showing boys controlling a miniature railroad while girls looked on. Similar images appeared on the boxes containing train sets. The idea was irresistible: More than a product,

Ives was selling an experience, the opportunity to operate a rail network like the Pennsylvania or the New York Central. Illustrations glorifying the elements of this system (trains, stations, track, and so forth) might sustain sales over more than one holiday season. Given sufficient diversity and promotion, a toy train line could appeal to a boy for several years before he tired of his railroad as adolescence beckoned.

Cohen, therefore, was not the first to develop a miniature electric train or to push his line through illustrated catalogs. But being first is not necessary if one can do something better. As Ives, Märklin, and others learned to their dismay, Cohen, as much an impresario as a tinkerer, found ways of beating them at their own games. His New York-based firm, which he named the Lionel Manufacturing Co., steadily rose to prominence in the early 1900s.

fortune and fame

Driving Cohen and invigorating early Lionel art were his dreams of success. He wanted to dominate the American toy train market. Illustrations, he knew, were essential to fulfilling his ambitions. Side views (known as "silhouettes") of individual items would attract customers; the descriptive verbiage that almost

text continues on page 26

Above: The theme of a boy operating a train while a girl sits and watches did not originate with Lionel. Ives, an early rival of Lionel's, used it, as seen on the cover of its 1910 catalog. So had German and French toy makers at least a decade earlier.

the influence of Ives

Whether in the design of Lionel trains or the composition of catalog artwork, Joshua Cowen made the Ives Manufacturing Corp. his point of reference. He set his sights on surpassing this established New England toy maker and eventually acquired most of his rival's assets when Ives declared bankruptcy in 1928. A gleeful Cowen later boasted—falsely—that he then dumped the Ives tooling in a river.

Right: Electrics and steamers barrel out of a metropolitan terminal in this picture, which appeared on the cover of the 1930 Ives catalog. The radiant colors belie the firm's desperate straits. Ives had filed for bankruptcy, and Lionel gained control of its trains. Cowen soon dispensed with these locomotives and sets, keeping only low-end windups and electrics.

The lucky lad on the wraparound front and back covers of the 1913 catalog must own every train and accessory in the Lionel line, plus its racing car set and battery-powered motors (running the gadgets to his right). Not for the last time will a younger sister be shunted to the side. Do you see the first Lionel mascot, to the right of the overhead light?

Lionel Electric Train On a Big Bridge

Built with the Famous Structural Steel Building Toy: MECCANO

$1000 MECCANO PRIZE CONTEST
Get entry Blank at your dealer's and win a prize.

Meccano Prices

Outfit No. 420. Pullman Train DeLuxe

Meccano and Lionel Electric Toys are sold at the best class of Toy and Department Stores, Electrical Stores, etc.

Complete with Electric Lights inside Cars, extra amount of Track, etc. *Buy It.*

Lionel art changed significantly after 1915. Previously, the firm had emphasized that its trains were playthings for young children. Now, to reach older boys who wanted realistic trains that reflected the world around them, artists depicted trains in urban, industrial scenes. The Standard gauge set crossing a suspension bridge delighted readers of the 1917 catalog.

smothered these images would clarify why Lionel products were best. Missing from art published before 1910 were references to either Lionel as a manufacturing enterprise or its founder. Neither was likely at this time to hold much sway. Besides, once Cohen had tasted success in this venture, he might repeat the past and move on to another electrical novelty, one with more commercial value and social prestige than miniature trains and elementary motors.

Thus, the earliest Lionel art served only to advertise what Cohen was crafting in the firm's cramped loft. Between 1901 and 1905, the motorized cars and open trolleys bearing the Lionel name ran on two-rail track with wooden ties and built to the unique gauge (i.e., distance between the rails) of $2^{7}/_{8}$ inches. That these

trains were not compatible with any other brand scarcely mattered to Cohen. He aimed only to make something different and promote it as better. If Lionel catalogs succeeded, consumers would not want to combine its trains with those manufactured by Ives, Bing, or Carlisle & Finch.

The same audacity influenced Cohen's decision to bring out a smaller type of train in 1906. Models ran on standardized, preassembled sections of three-rail straight and curved track with a gauge of $2^{1}/_{8}$ inches. Its width made it incompatible with any other brand. Some observers argue that Cohen intended for his trains to be *sui generis*. Others say he inadvertently ended up with something that could not be combined. The truth has vanished over time. Cohen never admitted that he had erred. A shrewd marketer,

he later proclaimed in catalogs that Lionel trains were the "standard of the world." All others were, by implication, inferior.

Catalogs backed up Cohen's claims about the excellence of his "Standard" gauge line. Their illustrations, functional rather than aesthetic in design, became larger and boasted more detail and finer shading after 1906. Lionel, for the first time in its history, showed "outfits" (a locomotive and cars). Doing so raised the appeal of these more expensive items and linked them in the public's mind with real passenger and freight trains. None of this represented a departure from what Ives or German toy makers were doing. Rather, changes in Lionel art offer insights into how Cohen's sales skills and his knowledge of the market were growing keener.

Further evidence appears in illustrations published in the 1910s, a watershed for Lionel. Critical changes took place, all related to a decision to produce miniature railroads that were toys and not retail displays. Once committed, Lionel set out to conquer the field. Cowen (the new name appeared in 1910, perhaps part of his bid to overtake the Yankees dominating the domestic toy industry) moved production to New Haven, Connecticut, not far from the Ives plant in Bridgeport. He also delegated authority, assigning Mario Caruso (an immigrant from Italy already at Lionel) to supervise the factory and hiring Mark Harris (a veteran in the toy field) to oversee sales.

The pictures in Lionel's catalogs took on a new look. For the first time, bright colors

The practice of making Lionel trains seem realistic by placing them in modern settings reached its peak in the 1950s. This illustration in the 1953 catalog shows incredible detail in the huge refinery or processing plant and the O gauge freight trains.

Once Cowen had leveled the playing field, he prepared to smash the competition by demostrating that his trains were superior. Lionel art changed again after World War I erupted in 1914 and German toy makers were frozen out of the American market. Lionel devoted its resources to besting Ives and holding at bay such challengers as American Flyer and Voltamp. Illustrations took on an aggressive tone that, while tame by current standards, must have taken the toy industry by surprise and left many insiders uncomfortable with Cowen's tactics.

His plan to dethrone Ives manifested itself in artwork that aimed to prove that Lionel trains were better. Cast-iron locomotives were shown shattering on impact with a hard floor while stamped sheet-metal ones suffered hardly a dent. Passenger cars decorated with lithography were derided as inferior and less realistic than those painted with enamels.

Since Ives used the scorned methods and Lionel the others, consumers had no trouble concluding which trains must be tougher and truer to life and, therefore, better suited for America's youth. These images revealed

Joshua Cowen inserted stylized images of his son in Lionel catalogs and on train set boxes in the late 1910s and early 1920s to remind children of how much fun they would have with his trains. Lawrence, to his father's delight, grew up to be president of Lionel.

distinguished the covers and children were shown playing with trains. Such scenes tied trains to a happy childhood, a theme already explored by Märklin and Ives. In fact, the subject was so far from original that a newcomer like the American Flyer Manufacturing Co. quickly adopted this approach. But the lack of originality was the point. No child or parent seeing Lionel art could imagine that its Standard gauge trains were different and thus not equal to others in quality and pleasure.

Cowen's understanding that to achieve pre-eminence in the field he had to broaden the appeal of his trains. Reaching the kids who would play with them with pictures of what he sold was not enough. He also had to persuade the adults who paid for the toys that his were the best.

the Lionel experience

Artwork from the 1910s sought as well to define toy trains as part of what might be called the "Lionel experience." This concept sheds light on prevailing ideas of childhood and the place of toys nearly a century ago. It begins with the premise—one that artists as well as Cowen would have accepted—that the appeal of miniature trains was limited to children. The idea that a boy might play with his trains well into adolescence or that an adult might see them as a legitimate leisure pursuit was scarcely considered because these were playthings inevitably cast aside.

This view of trains mirrored the emerging sense among the wealthy and highly educated in the early 20th century that childhood was a separate phase of life. According to this line of thinking, boys and girls should be left free to play and dream during their first ten or so years. Naturally, leisure and fantasy were expected to be

Two No. 26—14 Volt Lamps for Headlights.
Two No. 49—21 Volt Globes for Lamp Posts.
Two No. 48—21 Volt Lamps for Switches.
Price, *$135.00; †$160.00; ‡$197.50.

LIONEL OUTFIT No. 424
A COMPLETE ELECTRIC RAILROAD

* Price, East of Missouri River.
† Price, West of Missouri River.
‡ Price in Canada

carried out in ways that nurtured the values prized by the adult world. Toys assumed central roles in a fulfilling, productive childhood.

Cowen, aware of the importance of toys, set out to legitimize the appeal of his miniature trains. To achieve this goal and advance his fortunes, he turned again to art. Illustrations would show children that Lionel trains were fun while persuading adults that they were safe and constructive. Pictures of youngsters all but mesmerized while playing with their trains served both purposes.

The fact that these toys were electric was crucial in winning over kids and adults. Cowen knew only too well how infatuated his countrymen were with this dynamic, still mysterious form of energy. Electricity was something, his

text continues on page 32

Cowen and his sales manager, Mark Harris, realized by the time the 1920 catalog was released that business would improve if they showed consumers how much could be done with Lionel trains and accessories. Selling a station and tunnel, lights, and extra track with a set was one solution.

Above: Jacques Zuccaire prepared this sketch in pastel chalks for the cover of the 1953 catalog. He says that for final covers that included both trains and people, Lionel often commissioned different painters to handle the different subjects. This practice probably originated during the prewar era.

Below: Paul Smith (left) and Orlando Militano, art directors in Lionel's advertising department, confer over the final design of pages 24 and 25 of the 1959 catalog. They worked with advertising manager Jacques Zuccaire to prepare the sketches that cover the bulletin board.

art for the catalog

At least since the 1910s, the process of illustrating Lionel's annual catalog has involved several executives. Former advertising manager Jacques Zuccaire recalls that in a typical year in the 1950s he would bring Lawrence Cowen (then president of the firm) and Alan Ginsburg (executive vice-president) six sketches of potential covers. They made the final decision, and Zuccaire had a professional artist paint the cover. Meanwhile, his art director, Orlando Militano, assisted by Paul Smith, designed illustrations for the interior pages and assigned them to freelance artists employed by local advertising agencies.

This painting served as the basis for the cover of the 1957 catalog. A freelance artist designed it using models of trains and preliminary black-and-white sketches prepared by the Lionel advertising department.

catalog for 1913 promised, "the mechanically inclined boy will never tire of." One part of the Lionel experience was to connect inquisitive children with the world of electrical novelties that fascinated their elders.

Catalog illustrations didn't conceal the wires, batteries, and transformers that set the trains in motion. Quite the opposite. They glorified the "current reducers" and "new departure battery motors" that Lionel sold. Artwork, including the drawings used with the first advertisements that Lionel placed in mass-circulation magazines, suggested that boys took as much pride in operating an electric train as men did in owning the first electric range on the block.

But if one part of the experience depicted in Lionel catalogs linked kids to the world of their parents, another offered the chance to avoid it. "Lionel toys," the 1912 catalog stated, "instruct and amuse at the same time." With childhood seen as an innocent, less demanding part of life, toys took on greater meaning. Playthings ought to educate yet also elicit pleasure.

Lionel trains unquestionably brought joy into a child's life. The relaxed posture and broad smiles of the kids shown in illustrations left no doubt that having a set was terrific fun. Sitting on the floor, surrounded by hundreds of dollars worth of trains and accessories: these youngsters were in paradise. And not a parent, teacher, or minister in sight! Lionel trains were tickets for escaping the chores and lessons adults foisted on children.

Only one grown-up regularly appeared in Lionel art during the 1910s: Mr. Cowen himself. The balding gentleman shown was not the hard-driving entrepreneur scheming to crush all foes. No, this was the pal who, rare among adults, understood the burdens placed on boys. Starting in 1915, Cowen filled catalogs with photographs of his factory and invited readers to join him on a tour.

Though Cowen and his "boys" recognized that parents bought the trains, they still wanted to keep grown-ups out of the magical world of Lionel. Let adults occasionally visit, perhaps to admire the powerful engines and colorful cars or to acknowledge the inferiority of other brands. Otherwise, Cowen seemed ready to lock out his peers and assist boys in escaping the drudgery and rules associated with the adult world. His factory would be strictly for amusement, much like Coney Island or a darkened movie theater.

One boy seemed to reside in the land of Lionel. Beginning in 1914 and continuing for a decade, catalogs, ads, and boxes featured the image of a boy kneeling before a set. Drawings of a typical lad gave way to photographs of an actual boy, only to be succeeded by stylized illustrations of that same young man. Altogether three distinct images were used, each suggesting that this boy represented "Over a Million Satisfied Users." Kids glancing at catalogs and opening boxes of trains identified with the cover subject who, they imagined, was no stranger to the Lionel plant.

Truth be told, the lad whose photographed face was superimposed on the body drawn for the 1917 catalog had visited the factory. He had watched Lionel trains being made and shaken the hand of the affable Cowen. As for trains, this boy probably had more of them to race and destroy than any kid in America. Little Lawrence Cowen, nine or ten years old when his father first pictured him in a Lionel catalog, served as a model for every boy who dreamed of owning an outfit.

Cowen used his son in place of imaginary boys to prove that trains guaranteed pleasure

and guidance to America's youth. Granted, few observers knew the identity of the "Lionel boy." A photograph nonetheless seemed more real to viewers and strengthened Cowen's assertions about the value of his products. (It may also have bolstered his hope that he was succeeding as a father.)

As anyone looking at Lionel art realized, Cowen was not reluctant to entrust a boy with a Standard gauge set. He believed it would transform the youngster's life. Other parents should feel the same way because the Lionel experience offered entertainment, along with knowledge about electricity and railroads. Trains safely exposed children to the world around them and contributed to their education. Unlike other

This view of an enormous brick-and-glass structure in grassy fields, taken from the 1917 catalog, represented Cowen's dream more than it did the reality of the Lionel factory.

The Merriest Christmas of All—

Bright and early Christmas morning you and your boy will be running his Lionel Train, enjoying the "thrills" of the World's most fascinating and educational toy.

Lionel Trains and Miniature Railroad Equipment are exact reproductions of those used on America's leading railroad systems.

Lionel locomotives are powerful enough to haul a train of twenty or more cars around curves, through tunnels, over bridges and across switches.

The realistic Lionel equipment includes Crossing Gates that automatically lower as the train approaches and raise as it passes by. Electric Block Signals flash "Danger" and "Clear Track Ahead," while Electric Warning Signals ring at the crossings.

Lionel products have all the up-to-the-minute improvements in modern railroad design and construction. All Lionel Locomotives, Cars and Accessories are of steel construction and practically indestructible.

For 23 years Lionel Electric Trains have been electrically and mechanically perfect—fully guaranteed. They are attractively finished in rich enamels and baked like automobile bodies.

You can see Lionel Trains in operation at the best toy, hardware, electrical, sporting goods and department stores.

Complete Lionel Outfits sell from $5.75 up.

Send for the new 48-page Lionel catalogue—a handsome book showing the complete line in colors. It's Free!

THE LIONEL CORPORATION
Dept. 18, 48-52 East 21st Street, New York City
"Standard of the World" Since 1900

LIONEL ELECTRIC TOY TRAINS
& Multivolt Transformers

toys, a set might be considered a necessity as the pace of change accelerated in America following World War I.

factory in paradise

Joshua Cowen's dreams of success and the hopes he stirred in youngsters coalesced in illustrations of the Lionel factory, which had been located in and around Newark, New Jersey, since 1914. Gone were the black-and-white photographs of machine shops, with laborers toiling at die presses and test tracks, that had filled catalogs in 1915 and 1916. In their place in the late 1910s and early '20s was a color rendering of a huge, modern industrial facility. Automobiles and trucks motored by the brick-and-glass structure, passing pedestrians as the American flag fluttered in the breeze.

"Our Big Plant at Irvington, N. J." looked like a giant version of a Lionel accessory. Despite the plumes drifting out of smokestacks, the factory posed no threat. It wasn't a fortress or a symbol of urban blight. This facility, its entrance open to the public, fit into its pastoral setting and improved what nature had created. Viewers could almost hear the stamping machines thumping away and imagine contented laborers assembling and painting toys like elves at the North Pole.

Cowen must have taken comfort in this fanciful image of the factory. For it was a fantasy. Although Lionel had moved in 1917 to newer quarters in Irvington, not far from Newark, its plant was nowhere near the size of the one pictured in catalogs. Neither was the setting as bucolic and soothing. Boys admiring the illustration might be fooled, but Cowen knew the truth.

He could, however, dream of owning such a factory. Someday, Cowen surely vowed, his trains would be made in a facility more like the ones making Pullman coaches or Ford automobiles than the one making Ives trains. (Ironically, Ives catalogs from the early 1920s contained exaggerated images of its plant.) Until then, let the public imagine that his products came from so grand a site. Let competitors fear that Lionel was expanding so fast it would outgrow even this fictitious structure.

Cowen's ambitions, regardless of how much they had been fulfilled by 1921, continued to drive him. Never did he relinquish the dream of dominating the toy field while showing the public that his company had importance beyond that minor area. His counterparts at Ives might be satisfied as toy makers, but Cowen really wanted to stand at the forefront of the production of electrical items. His miniature trains should be seen, no longer as novelties, but as appliances that entertained and enlightened the boys playing with them and reassured the parents buying them.

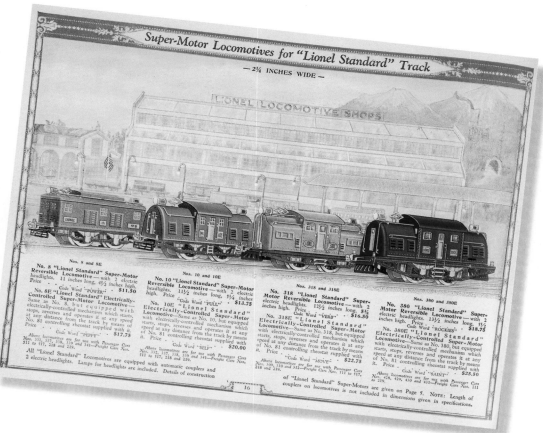

Cowen's perception of his role as inventor and marketer and his firm's role in touching the lives of both children and adults influenced early Lionel art. Whether depicting trains, children, Cowen, or the factory, illustrations reinforced the image that owners of Lionel products entered into a relationship with the man at the helm. They earned Cowen's respect and friendship; seeking his approval, they would buy more trains and bolster a link that was more than just commercial in nature. It had a personal side because, as he reminded the readers of his catalogs, "Lionel" was his middle name.

Picturing the cream of the Standard gauge motive power pool in front of a massive structure labeled "Lionel Locomotive Shops" bolstered the claim that Lionel trains were like real ones. This striking illustration graced the 1927 catalog and must have influenced the dreams of so many children before the holidays.

chapter two

Dreams of consumption
1920-1933

By the 1920s, Lionel was on its way to eclipsing Ives as the leading toy train maker in America. It was also holding off challenges posed by American Flyer and the newcomers Boucher and Dorfan as well as any efforts by German firms to regain a share of the market. The success of Lionel brought material comforts to Cowen. Yet he had no desire to be seen as a toy baron. He wanted his business and social peers to hold him in higher esteem. Never forgetting his earliest dreams, Cowen emphasized in art and advertising that his company made miniature trains powered by the magic of electricity. "The day of 'toy' trains is past," declared the catalog for 1925. "Lionel Model Electric Trains, faithful reproductions of the massive locomotives and cars used on America's great electrified systems, have replaced them." Rather than compare Lionel to Ives or American Flyer, Cowen seemed to think that the public should associate his firm with Westinghouse or General Electric.

The perception that Lionel models were appliances sure to entertain survived from earlier years to influence illustrations in the 1920s. So did the idea that those trains were part of an experience that enriched childhood. Cowen, to feed his ambitions and broaden the appeal of his trains, redefined the Lionel experience to include older boys. His trains were instrumental in shaping character and charting destiny, or so art suggested. Such an approach would capture boys on the verge of adolescence without alienating Lionel's traditional customer base of younger kids and their families.

Cowen's efforts manifested themselves in art that enlivened catalogs and magazine ads. Illustrations used after 1921 shied away from implying that Lionel products were suited for young children only. Similarly, they avoided portraying trains as exclusively vehicles of escape or elements in a youthful world cut off from that inhabited by parents and teachers. Art reflected a new attitude at Lionel; namely, that

it was shortsighted to imagine that boys inevitably abandoned their electric trains for pursuits deemed more mature and seen as preludes to higher education and jobs.

Why should boys cast aside their trains when, as Lionel art insisted, operating miniature locomotives and cars prepared them to enter the world of their fathers? Links between owning trains and becoming a man emerged as conceptions of masculinity were shifting. The idea that buying such playthings could influence a boy's future says much about the rise of a consumer culture that proclaims the virtues of acquisition

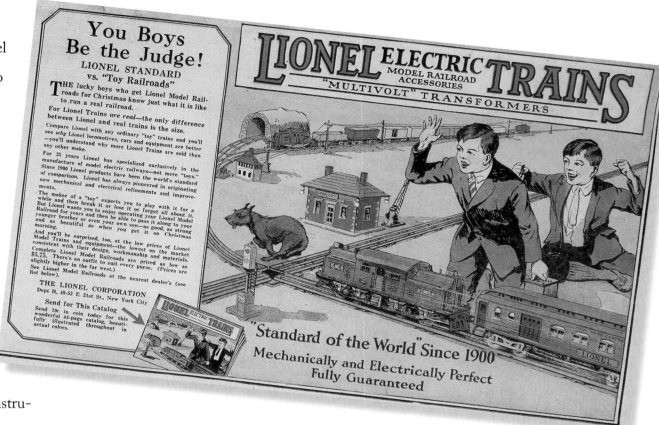

The "Lionel experience" became something boys of all ages could enjoy in the 1920s. No matter how much fun they were having, they still dressed as their fathers would have, as shown in this ad in the comics of the *Syracuse Sunday American* of December 7, 1924.

HERE IS THE WONDER TRAIN OF MODERN TIMES—THE REAL THING—IN MINIATURE
PASSENGER TRAIN OUTFIT No. 403 WITH "TWIN-SUPER-MOTOR" LOCOMOTIVE FOR "STANDARD" GAUGE TRACK—2¼ INCHES WIDE

Large renderings of Standard gauge outfits that faithfully portrayed the details on these trains weren't common. However, as this two-page spread from the 1923 catalog shows, they were bound to impress consumers.

and not productivity. Changes in the look and presentation of Lionel models reflected and advanced the popular beliefs in consumption that rule American life.

classic trains and art

The development of the Lionel line made it easier for Cowen and his associates to convince the public that their trains should always be part of a boy's life. Starting in 1923, the Standard gauge roster underwent significant changes. Technological advances in production proceeded hand in hand with innovations in design to help Lionel manufacture trains and accessories that, according to some collectors, have never been surpassed.

Larger locomotives equipped with more powerful motors made their debut. They pulled rolling stock that, thanks to advances in stamping steel and mixing and applying enamel paints, had never been so sturdy or attractive.

Freight and passenger cars made after 1923 featured gleaming trim to accentuate their colors (terra cotta, olive, Mojave, peacock, maroon, and apple green, among others). Coaches and observation cars came with two-tone paint schemes and gold lettering. Their hinged roofs swung open to reveal interior lights and details ranging from seats to commodes.

Equally outstanding were the accessories. Designed in Italy and manufactured in New Jersey, these items included flashing block signals and semaphores, a bridge modeled after the Hell Gate Bridge in New York City, and various stations, the largest of which were based on actual urban terminals. A huge industrial facility suggested the factory that Cowen had dreamed of owning. Most glorious, at least from an artistic perspective, were the hand-painted tunnels.

Prices were not rock bottom. Cowen had no desire to imitate Henry Ford and offer a toy train for every wallet. Instead, as catalog illustrations show, Cowen wanted to create the impression that his products belonged in a higher echelon than did his competitors'. He had been doing so since promoting electric trains and ignoring interest in windups. Art was integral to Cowen's strategy of having the masses meet his expectations rather than reaching down to theirs.

Superb artwork complemented the new trains and showed off their many advantages. Illustrations captured the dreams of boys and then, like movies or dime novels, supplied youngsters with the stuff of their next fantasy. Pictures in catalogs left young consumers eager to own the finest Lionel set in town and wishing they could operate it in a spacious home where electricity and parental approval were equally abundant. Vivid images taught boys that the right toys ensured happiness and eased the pathway to manhood. Wishing (what some observers condemned as coveting) was not harmful; even envy could be beneficial. "Aspire to have the best," Mr. Cowen might have advised.

Through its art, Lionel set out to impress upon boys and their families that its trains and

accessories were the best. Personal appeals from Cowen disappeared, as did photographs demonstrating the inferiority of rival brands. Instead, after 1920 Lionel relied on realistic yet evocative pictures to whet the appetites of kids. The images filling catalog covers were more imaginative than most of their predecessors. Artists used novel compositions and their entire palette to create memorable scenes in which trains alternate between being the stars and serving as props for human models of different ages.

Never before had Lionel trains seemed so big and lively. Professional illustrators, whether employees of agencies or freelancers, reached deep into their bag of techniques and talents to convey the speed, heft, and authority of new sets and accessories. The range of colors they used rivaled the spectrum that the paint

text continues on page 42

Standard and O gauge Scenic Railways, which made their debut in the 1924 catalog, carried on Lionel's tradition of displays. Beautiful backdrops and hand-painted tunnels were major attractions of these layouts.

39

Raymond L. Thayer (1887-1955), an illustrator best known for capturing the rural beauty of New England and Virginia in watercolors, painted this domestic scene. It was used in an ad in the December 1922 *Scribner's* before filling the cover of the 1923 catalog. Thayer reveals how the wealthy, living in spacious homes with sumptuous furnishings, enjoyed their Lionel trains.

to be young in the '20s

Besides showing us the finest Standard gauge trains, art from the 1920s sheds light on what it meant to be a boy so long ago. Lionel catalog and magazine illustrations portrayed them as miniature men, just as they depicted trains as small versions of real railroad equipment. Lying on a floor or standing next to a table, boys dressed in white shirts and ties studiously operated their trains. Their eyes, dark and bright, convey joy as well as gravity. In their minds these boys are engineers responsible for getting the local express into town on schedule. These pictures, done by experienced artists, seem timeless because the facial expressions hardly differ from those we see on children now as they lose themselves in play.

Above: Clothes might make the man, but as this sales brochure from 1925 proves, the smile makes the boy, especially when he's the owner of a new Lionel passenger set. Bertram Goodman (1904-1988) painted this warm illustration, which his Uncle Josh (Cowen, that is) was only too glad to use for promoting the Standard gauge line.

Left: Joseph Adda (1893-1980), a commercial artist in New York, used his son as a model for the cover of the catalog for 1929. Rather than create an elaborate living room with networks of tracks and elegant furniture, Adda reduced the scene to one boy and two trains. He was thus able to enlarge the sets and add the details that entranced young consumers.

A BEAUTIFUL NEW LIONEL STATION—COMPLETELY ILLUMINATED

LIONEL CITY

The magnificence of the no. 129 platform and the no. 128 station perched upon it comes through in this picture from the 1928 catalog. Adding to the glamor is the illuminated passenger train dashing by at twilight, with silhouetted trees and houses behind it.

department at Lionel sprayed on thousands of models. Artists banished the silhouettes of trains they had formerly executed. Now they depicted locomotives barreling forward, headlights blazing and flags fluttering. They experimented with a host of angles, as though one were looking down on trains from a walkway or up at them from trackside. The effect was liberating and thrilling.

Noteworthy, too, was the practice of placing Lionel trains in more diverse settings. Where an artist posed a set or two depended on the message he wanted to convey. By showing three-rail track crisscrossing a floor in a 1922 illustration, Raymond L. Thayer highlighted the enjoyment a child could have with what was

obviously a miniature railroad. There was nothing unusual about this technique; catalog art and labels on boxes had featured similar scenes since the late 19th century.

However, to grab the attention of older boys and underscore the realism of Lionel trains, artists blended trains and accessories into contemporary urban and rural scenes. Standard gauge freight cars waited on a siding next to a factory. Smaller O gauge passenger sets chugged by farms and through hills. The Lionel Hell Gate Bridge stood on craggy stone piers while ships plied the waters below.

Who could blame viewers if they found it difficult to discern whether a locomotive or a powerhouse was life-sized or a replica? Sowing such confusion was the purpose behind fitting playthings into outdoor scenery. That's why the 1928 catalog announced, "Lionel Railroading is an Exciting Game! . . . Because it's so real!" Artists, too, wanted consumers to feel that operating a Lionel train was just like managing an actual railroad. It was work that had to be taken seriously and handled responsibly like a man, with cool nerves, steady hands, and an organized mind.

more than trains

Accurate, dramatic depictions of trains testify to improvements in Lionel art. So do the portraits of kids and adults. Showing boys playing with trains and letting their imaginations soar, a technique used infrequently prior to 1920, became the rule after 1923. In place of Lawrence Cowen leaning over a set, children appeared in different poses. Sometimes they lounged on the floor, while at others times they stood by the track or alongside a tunnel. On occasion, a boy played alone; more often, pairs of youngsters were shown. Where once a girl would have watched as her brother ran the train, now a younger boy sat by as an older one handled the transformer. The implication was clear: Lionel trains were for boys, especially mature ones able to appreciate their beauty and merit.

Artists reinforced this point in another way. Years before in Lionel and Ives illustrations, children looked like children. The little engineers were rosy-cheeked lads with mounds of curls who wore sailor suits. Lawrence Cowen ended this style. He dressed in a wool suit, his dark hair slicked down like a man's. Youths pictured afterwards in the mid-1920s through the early '30s carried this trend forward. Advertisements and catalog images showed boys

text continues on page 46

Working with Lionel trains demanded concentration and agility—just look at the boys' hands and eyes. The pleasures these models brought were immense, as Fernando E. Ciavatti showed in the cover of the 1928 catalog.

43

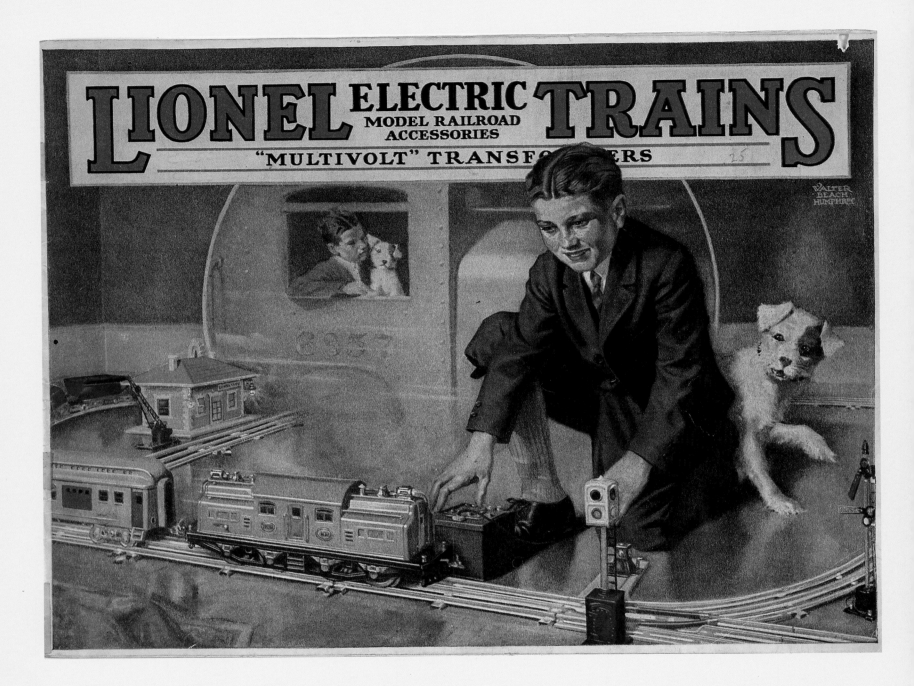

Every boy who has handled the controls of a
Lionel train has pretended that he's sitting at
the throttle of a mighty locomotive, maybe with
his dog Patches or Sandy in his lap. Few illustrations depicted this fantasy better than the
cover of the 1925 catalog, as painted by
Walter Beach Humphrey.

Humphrey's boys

The smiles and relaxed gestures of the boys painted by Walter Beach Humphrey (1892-1966) perfectly express the pleasures of running an electric train. No artist in the prewar era matched this celebrated muralist and magazine illustrator at depicting the interaction between children and trains. Whether dressed to the nines or wearing knickers and pullovers, the young men in Humphrey's art seem to feel comfortable and happy. Such details as wrinkles in their pants and hair that was a bit messy made it easier for real boys to identify with them.

Walter Beach Humphrey, who enjoyed a long and distinguished career as a commercial artist and teacher of art, painted evocative illustrations of boys playing with their Lionel sets. This boy, with his wide grin and rumpled shirt, seems to be having the time of his life in this view, which distinguished a 1926 sales brochure.

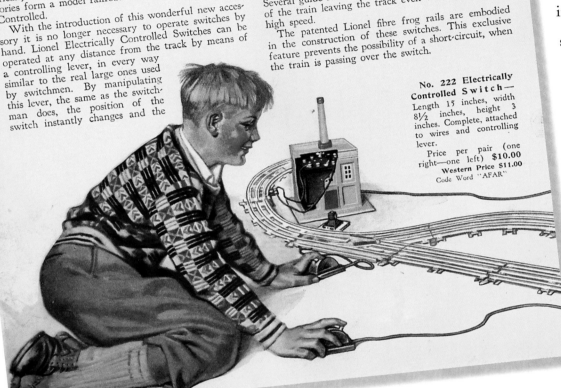

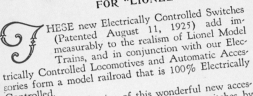

The New Electrically Controlled Switches
FOR "LIONEL STANDARD" TRACK—2¼ INCHES WIDE

THESE new Electrically Controlled Switches (Patented August 11, 1925) add immeasurably to the realism of Lionel Model Trains, and in conjunction with our Electrically Controlled Locomotives and Automatic Accessories form a model railroad that is 100% Electrically Controlled.

With the introduction of this wonderful new accessory it is no longer necessary to operate switches by hand. Lionel Electrically Controlled Switches can be operated at any distance from the track by means of a controlling lever, in every way similar to the real large ones used by switchmen. By manipulating this lever, the same as the switchman does, the position of the switch instantly changes and the red and green lights in the switch lantern change with the movement of the switch. The controlling lever is permanently connected with the switch by means of flexible wires so that no additional wiring is required.

The mechanism of Lionel Electrically Controlled Switches is extremely simple. There is nothing to get out of order. They are scientifically constructed. Several guide rails are used to eliminate the possibility of the train leaving the track even when operating at high speed.

The patented Lionel fibre frog rails are embodied in the construction of these switches. This exclusive feature prevents the possibility of a short-circuit, when the train is passing over the switch.

No. 222 Electrically Controlled Switch— Length 15 inches, width 8½ inches, height 3 inches. Complete, attached to wires and controlling lever.
Price per pair (one right—one left) $10.00
Western Price $11.00
Code Word "AFAR"

Here's another of the relaxed young men that inhabited the world created by Walter Beach Humphrey. Seeing this illustration from the 1926 catalog leaves us feeling that we know the kid (isn't he named Bobby or Jack?) and the fun he's having with a Lionel train.

dressed in apparel that made them look like miniature adults on their way to the office. Boys sported white shirts, dark ties, and buttoned-down jackets because running a Lionel train was serious business. Conservative clothes and stern demeanors were required, just as they were for men supervising factory hands or selling merchandise.

Even when artists showed boys at leisure, their subjects seemed older and worldlier than before. One illustrator, Walter Beach Humphrey, specialized in preadolescents relaxing with Lionel sets. In fact, Lionel may have requested him because, as the covers he painted for *Saturday Evening Post*, *American Boy*, and other magazines reveal, Humphrey, like his contemporary Norman Rockwell, was a master at portraying boys at play or earnestly dealing with adults. In his work for Lionel, boys decked out in striped pullovers and knickers sprawled on the floor next to a set. Thoroughly engrossed in controlling their train, they seemed a bit tense. Their expressions resembled those of adults about to smack a tennis ball or rein in a polo pony.

Through their artwork, Lionel insisted that a miniature railroad, once seen as only fun and escape for young children, could educate and shape a boy's character. Lionel trains, the catalog for 1924 promised its readers, "will give you a knowledge of the principles of electricity . . .

help you solve problems in traction and transportation . . . knowledge that will be of inestimable value to you when you grow to manhood." If, as one firm claimed, "Ives Toys Make Happy Boys," then Cowen might have countered with "Lionel Trains Build Future Brains."

Where illustrations of Lionel trains appeared was as important as how those toys and the individuals using them were portrayed. The most familiar sources were the company's catalogs. Splendid pictures embellished the description of virtually every item in them. Department stores and electrical shops distributed huge numbers of catalogs. Other copies were mailed direct from Lionel headquarters to kids around the world. The lavishly illustrated wish books were treasured for generations.

But Cowen was too shrewd to rely exclusively on catalogs to reach consumers. He had been advertising in mass-circulation magazines since 1914 and trade publications still longer. Targeting vast audiences of children and adults, he broadened Lionel's presence in the 1920s.

Black-and-white images as well as full-color art appeared in *Boys' Life*, *Youth's Companion*, and *American Boy*. Adults, mothers as much as dads, were exposed to pictures of the latest sets and accessories in *Collier's*, *Literary Digest*, *Current Events*, *Popular Mechanics*, and *Liberty*, among many other popular magazines.

text continues on page 50

The illustrated label pasted onto the box of this Standard gauge outfit from 1928 brims over with images of boys having fun with their trains. Though these youngsters differ in age and dress, the wide smiles show the happiness they share.

The magnificent centerfold in the 1927 catalog would have been right at home in the original *Vanity Fair*. It used a popular illustrative style of the Roaring Twenties to depict the Standard gauge no. 409E Deluxe Model Express Train, its lights aglow, roaring through a darkened metropolis.

metropolitan skyline

Artists experimented with a variety of urban and industrial scenes as the backdrops for top-of-the-line items in the late 1920s and '30s. Their finest work evoked the wonders of Lionel's base of New York City. These illustrations could have doubled as travel posters to lure visitors to the jewel of the Empire State, then home to Babe Ruth, Al Jolson, and King Kong! Trains never looked as swank as they did when shown knifing their way by skyscrapers and the lights of Broadway and Park Avenue.

Above: Can't you hear the wheels of taxis squealing as cabbies rush to get to Grand Central Terminal before their passengers miss their trains? This graceful illustration from the 1928 catalog showcased the lamp posts Lionel offered so young engineers could design station scenes.

Left: The river below and the factory beyond are barely perceptible in this illustration of the no. 300 Hell Gate Bridge in the 1928 catalog. Even the approaching train seems unimportant. Only the new accessory, so grand and strong, matters. It dominates the scene like a monarch's crown.

No. 300 Steel Bridge
For "Lionel Standard" Track—2¼ Inches Wide

NOTHING so elaborate or architecturally perfect as this bridge has ever been made for use with a model electric train. It is faithfully modeled after the famous "Hell-gate" Bridge which spans the East River in New York. The piers, center span and structural features are correct to the minutest detail. It is made entirely of sheet steel, and is substantially constructed throughout. It measures 28½ inches in length, 11 inches in height and is 10½ inches wide. It is so skillfully designed that it is not necessary for a train to travel up or down grade when passing over it. It is finished in lasting enamel colors, and will greatly add to every boy's "Lionel Standard" Railroad Equipment. Price
Code Word "HELGA" $15.00

THE LIONEL MAGAZINE

The Model Railroad Magazine for Every Boy

IN THIS ISSUE: THE GEORGIA DYNAMITERS
PLANS FOR BUILDING MINIATURE GRAIN ELEVATOR

Lionel launched its own magazine in 1930 in hopes of increasing sales and promoting the nascent hobby of model railroading. This charming Christmas scene appeared on the cover of the November-December 1934 issue.

Lionel placed color ads in these supplements almost every November and December to encourage kids to request a set or at least a tank car or crossing gate as a holiday gift.

Cowen took a more audacious step in 1930. Taking a tip from another maker of toys, he launched his own magazine with guidance from advertising executive Joseph Hanson. Just as A.C. Gilbert had used the publication *Erector Tips* to generate enthusiasm for his Erector sets, so did Cowen use *Lionel Magazine* to introduce new models and teach readers how to run trains and build scenes for them. Color illustrations and black-and-white photographs distinguished this bimonthly publication. Superb images, including some associating Lionel train sets with Christmas, graced its front cover.

Launching a magazine and subsidizing more advertisements and bigger catalogs attest to Cowen's commitment to expanding his market. He depended on artwork to enhance the appeal of Lionel trains, regardless of whether the illustrations adorned magazine pages, newspapers, or cardboard displays and window trim shipped to hardware dealers and general merchandisers. The diverse sources of art show Cowen's

Determined to spread the gospel of electric trains to more kids and the parents anxious to please them, Cowen searched for other places to show off his trains. Eye-catching illustrations first added panache to the comics sections of Sunday newspapers in 1921. From then on,

willingness to devote more of his firm's budget to promotion, even if that involved contracts with higher-paid artists.

The quality of images supports this point, as do the signatures on catalog covers and ads. Raymond Thayer, Fernando E. Ciavatti, Jon O. Brubaker, and Bertram Goodman (a nephew of Cowen's) contributed distinctive illustrations that still delight.

Irrespective of who executed a particular illustration, what makes certain images memorable is the interaction they show between people and technology. Youngsters do more than simply play with toy trains in these pictures. They imagine, and they dream. As for the kids clutching a catalog and staring at the cover, they empathize with the boy shown trying to impress his father or the younger child fretting that he won't get a turn at the transformer. Lionel artwork captured the hopes and worries of youngsters and left them believing that a set was essential to happiness.

trains make the man

Happiness meant, of course, growing up to be a productive man known for his thrift, loyalty, honesty, and competence. Following the correct paths and meeting the right people enabled a

boy to assimilate the traits that would earn respectability and success. Sermons and school assignments taught valuable lessons, as did chores and discipline, all preparing lads to enter the working world. Boys from middle- and upper-income households took part in an

Winning the services of a painter as skilled as Jon O. Brubaker (1875–?) testified to how successful Lionel had become by the time this illustration appeared as part of an ad in the November 1928 *Boys' Life*.

The illustrations in ads from 1930 (December *Boys' Life*, left, and November *Popular Science*) were signed "M Bolgay." Using watercolors, this artist drew attention to the technical aspects of Lionel's products. You can't miss the enormous driving rod (left) or the crane car's delicate latticework (right).

"apprenticeship for manhood" that included playthings and activities geared toward transforming them into citizens of the future.

Lionel trains were elements of this phase because they promised knowledge of electricity and transportation. Until the 1920s, however, artwork had focused more on the amuse-

ment trains afforded young boys than the information and experience offered older ones. Cowen adjusted the emphasis so illustrations underlined the benefits trains had in preparing older boys to fulfill their dreams and enter a rapidly changing man's world.

It was not an easy sell. Electric trains were

wonderful fun for young boys, but when those fellows reached a certain age, say 11 or 12, they were expected to pack up their Lionel outfits or hand them down to a younger brother or cousin. Exceptions were shut-ins debilitated by illness or cerebral little professors, neither of whom had the stamina and muscles to engage in the strenuous activities that society recommended as training for manhood.

Sports and Scouting were the accepted ways for preadolescents to spend the hours when they weren't at school. These activities, connected with the outdoors, physical exertion, competition, and male mentors, inculcated the values of masculinity traditionally lauded in America. A culture that idolized Teddy Roosevelt, Jack Dempsey, General Pershing, and Tarzan scoffed at toy trains. Sitting on the floor watching a set chase itself around a loop of track was for sissies.

The challenge facing Lionel executives was how to overcome the prevailing view that electric trains had no value to boys struggling to tie square knots and wallop home runs. Unlike their counterparts at American Flyer, who capitalized on the name and inserted eagles and the Stars and Stripes in illustrations, Cowen and his staff did not associate their trains with patriotism. Instead, they reminded consumers in advertisements and catalog art and text that operating a

text continues on page 56

"Lionel Standard" Operating Derrick and Dump Cars

FOR USE WITH ALL LOCOMOTIVES OPERATING ON "LIONEL STANDARD" TRACK—2¼ INCHES WIDE

No. 219 Operating Derrick Car

BOYS—here is the most realistic railroad Derrick Car ever built in miniature. Think of the fun you will have operating it just like a real derrick. You can raise or lower the boom, swing it from side to side, and hoist weights with the pulley and tackle. In fact, this Derrick Car will do everything—the same as real ones. All mechanical movements are controlled by levers that operate worm gears. The mechanical arrangement is absolutely similar to that found in large Derrick Cars. By means of the worm gear the position of the boom and location of the boom are always in a rigid position, weights that are lowered or raised. They are always in a rigid position, except when changed by means of the levers. The mechanism is mounted on a solid steel car—11¾ inches long, 5⅜ inches high. The boom is 16 inches long. Car is equipped with automatic couplers. Price $8.50
Code Word "ALUM"

No. 218 Operating Dump Car

Bring up a load of sand or ballast, boys! We must finish that roadbed by to-morrow and run the first Lionel Limited over the new short cut. The new Lionel Operating Dump Car is a marvel of mechanical ingenuity. Not only does it look like the real cars used in the construction of railroads, but it actually dumps the load at any place desired along the track. The mechanical movements that automatically open and tilt the sides of the car are controlled by levers and worm gears. The Lionel Operating Dump Car is 11¾ inches long, 4½ inches high. Entirely constructed of sheet steel and beautifully finished by Lionel's famous enameling process. Equipped with automatic couplers. Price $5.85
Code Word "DEPEW"

Plenty of Standard gauge derrick and dump cars must have made their way on to lists for Santa Claus in 1927, once kids caught a glimpse of this awesome image in the catalog for that year. The sturdy, colorful models looked even bolder when juxtaposed against the illustration of their full-sized brethren at work.

Lionel created this window trim to enhance
sales of its Standard gauge line in 1930.
Times were tough, but retailers found room for
the cardboard representations of three impressive accessories.

giants and banners

Joshua Cowen launched his company as a manufacturer of window displays. Although he soon recognized the appeal of his trains as amusements for children and families, he never forgot that colorful, animated displays increased sales. By the 1920s, Lionel's advertising and display departments were developing signs, window trim, counter displays, banners, and layouts for retailers. They continued to offer more of these sales aids over the next 40 years so that in the "pre-television era" consumers could experience the thrills of toy trains.

Above: Shelf displays, layouts, and signs and banners nurtured dreams during the postwar era. What boy wouldn't beg for a Lionel set after seeing "The Giant of the Rails" in a toy or department store in 1950?

Left: Wall posters whetted everyone's appetite for the trains soon to arrive. William Bonanno, supervisor of the Lionel display department, painted the dynamic scene that was used for a 16-foot-long poster in 1954.

idea that owning a Lionel train demanded a great deal from a boy, most of all a sharp mind to grasp the details of running a railroad. Like a civil engineer, he learned to check his track and allow sufficient clearance under bridges. Like the conductor of a locomotive, he needed to obey signals and service his engines on schedule. Like a railroad executive, he had to ship freight and move passengers safely and expeditiously.

Unlike Lionel, whose catalog covers tended in the 1920s to show children playing with toy trains, the 1928 consumer catalog of the rival American Flyer Manufacturing Co. featured a top passenger set dashing across a majestic landscape with an eagle soaring.

Lionel outfit required concentration, forethought, and knowledge. Artists depicted larger, more elaborate setups than before. What kids saw on most catalog covers were railroad networks, miniature versions of the Pennsylvania or the Boston & Maine assembled on the floor of a living room or attic.

Pictures brimming over with locomotives, rolling stock, stations, and wires reinforced the

A train set should be far more than a toy. "You must think of the Lionel Corporation as a national institution of learning," argued the catalog for 1930. Illustrations showed that a Lionel outfit was part of a boy's education, teaching him the values and habits that guaranteed success.

But that was in the boy's future. For the present, a Lionel set offered something richer, the greatest prize any boy could dream of. The lad who operated his trains in a careful, realistic manner would earn the approval and enjoy the companionship of his father. This promise rippled through catalog and advertising text ("You can make him your assistant and bring him back to his boyhood days," stated the 1923 catalog). Yet it rarely influenced illustrations. Art might show a father dropping his paper to watch his son play, but he wasn't ready to help Junior build a three-rail empire. All the same, Cowen went on claiming that owning a set tightened the bonds between fathers and sons.

Consumption lay at the heart of the Lionel campaign. Buying more trains and adding them to a rapidly expanding home railroad would unite fathers and sons. Productivity—building that miniature system—was hardly mentioned in the 1920s. Here Cowen spurned traditional values of hard work and thrift. He played on hopes and fears to coax middle- and upper-income families into spending money on trains that would guide their sons toward adulthood. He knew the audience Lionel had to reach was less likely than earlier generations to condemn the purchase of consumer goods, including toys and

appliances, as harmful to a person's character. It saw the advantages of acquiring goods that made life more enjoyable and elevated them above their neighbors.

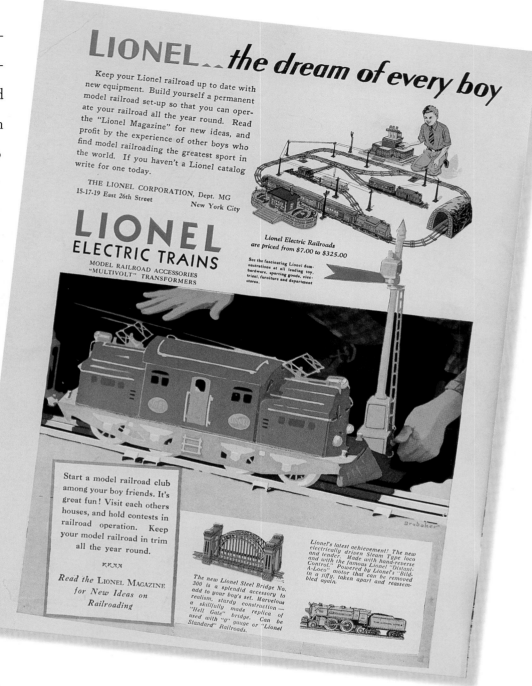

Standard gauge trains inspire dreams in this advertisement, painted by Jon O. Brubaker, in the May-June 1930 issue of *Lionel Magazine*.

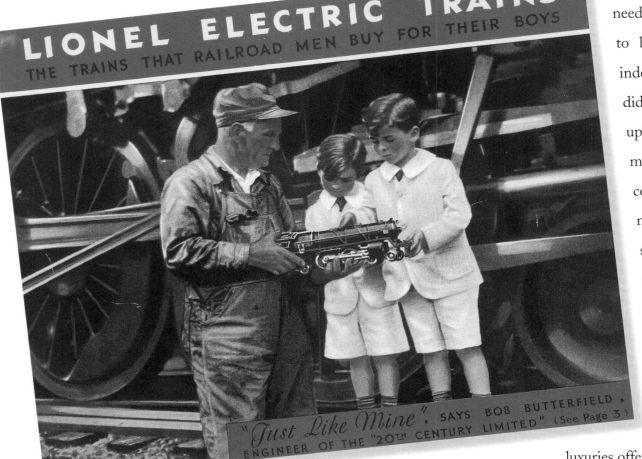

LIONEL ELECTRIC TRAINS
THE TRAINS THAT RAILROAD MEN BUY FOR THEIR BOYS

"Just Like Mine", SAYS BOB BUTTERFIELD, ENGINEER OF THE "20TH CENTURY LIMITED" (See Page 3)

The pressed white suits worn by this locomotive engineer's grandsons contrast with his wrinkled coveralls. No matter. As shown on the cover of the 1931 catalog, he was a hero whose endorsement validated the realism of Lionel trains.

The benefits of consumption were most obvious when, as Lionel art demonstrated, the items advertised contributed to a boy's social and education development. Electric trains, once peripheral to that phase of a young man's life, were now portrayed as key elements. Any family that hesitated to consume and refused to buy a set compromised their son's prospects. That could be disastrous at a time when notions of masculinity were changing. Boys

needed to feel that they could grow up to be productive, enterprising, and independent, even though more jobs did not call for those traits and did not uphold traditional views of what it meant to be a man. Lionel trains could not be ignored at so critical a moment, not when dreams of consumption promised to relieve worries about the future.

a new hero

But consumption proved ineffective if not impossible when the national economy collapsed in 1929. Buying conveniences and luxuries offered no hope for the millions of men losing their jobs and struggling to provide basic necessities for their families. Men were failing to live up to their traditional roles, and their sons could only look away and search for new heroes.

Lionel art reflected this sad turn of events. Even when times were hard, illustrations insisted on the benefits of an electric train for boys with enough pluck and determination to forge ahead. No matter how their fathers were faring, kids like this might succeed if they had someone productive and dependable to emulate. Lionel offered

IT'S 1928. AND YOU'VE JUST BECOM E THE
MOST POPULAR KID ON THE BL OCK.

It happened when you opened the box. You were finally the engineer of your very own Lionel freight train. And it was real. Just like the trains in the freight yard you'd sit and watch for hours. Magic. And suddenly, there were new friends everywhere.

Today, you can relive those glorious early days of Lionel

with Lionel Classics,™ authentic standard gauge recreations of the most famous Lionel trains ever built.

Journey back to the Twenties and Thirties with the Freight Express from Lionel, featuring the handsome

#1-318E loco-motive with Bild-A-Loco® motor and #500 series style rolling stock; black flatcar with real wood load; famous orange Shell tank car; rare blue and ivory refrigerator boxcar; and low-cupola caboose. Each piece displays the same craftsmanship and attention to detail as the originals. And there are other Lionel Classics: The historic Blue

Comet; the polished brass and nickel-plated "Old No. 7"; and introducing the fiery-red Fireball Express, a Lionel classic-in-the-making. Each painstakingly recreated and handcrafted, then given a shiny, baked-enamel finish with original style brass and nickel-plated accents. Be a part of the rich Lionel past with a train you'll treasure long into the future. Ask your Lionel dealer about Lionel Classics.

© 1990
Lionel Trains Inc.

LIONEL CLASSICS ™

---

them new heroes: locomotive engineers. Operating a miniature train was the best way to follow in their footsteps, especially when engineers declared in the 1931 and '32 catalogs that they bought only Lionel sets for their sons.

Illustrations showed why these were "The Trains That Railroad Men Buy for Their Boys." They featured Lionel trains in real-life settings and made those miniatures seem

larger, faster, and heavier. In the early 1930s, art (generally retouched photographs) carried the illusions further by posing actual engineers with Lionel models and having boys sit in the cab of mighty steam engines. Railroad men, from chief executives to locomotive drivers, replaced fathers as the adults young consumers should seek to emulate as they pretended their sets were the *Broadway Limited*.

No, it's not 1928. It's 1990 and the concept of popularity influences this advertisement for Lionel's Standard gauge reissues in the December *Classic Toy Trains* magazine. Decades earlier, when Lionel insisted that its trains brought out the best in a young man, character, rather than personality or popularity, would have been the theme of this ad.

59

chapter three
Dreams of authority
1931-1947

Art remained cheery as the Great Depression worsened. Meanwhile, sales at Lionel plummeted and the firm lost money every year from 1931 to 1933. Illustrations still promoted trains as essential to a boy's welfare ("see for yourself how much fun and valuable training a Lionel Model Railroad will give you," advised the 1934 catalog), but families trying to stay afloat financially judged electric trains to be luxuries well beyond their means. The firm that had looked robust at the end of the 1920s was in desperate straits. Joshua Cowen, who later confessed that he had intended to retire in 1929, watched his losses mount. He had every right to complain about his fate and lash out at consumers.

Cowen did not. Whatever he felt in his heart and said to confidants, the side he showed the public remained optimistic. As proof, look at Lionel art from the early 1930s. It went on depicting top-of-the-line outfits in vibrant tones. American Flyer, in contrast, economized by reprinting on its catalog cover images of full-sized trains borrowed from railroads. Lionel trains remained huge and glamorous in its art. Boys seeing these pictures would have found it difficult to surrender their dreams of finding a set wrapped under a Christmas tree or propped next to a birthday cake.

Cowen did not let go of his dreams either. If the products developed and the images created between 1934 and 1947 are indications, he carried his hopes for himself and his firm into newer and more ambitious realms. During the early history of Lionel, Cowen had used illustrations to promote the notion that he was making sophisticated playthings that introduced boys to the adult world and shaped their character. Lionel electrical novelties helped young

men earn approval from their fathers and let them feel they were the friends of locomotive engineers and railroad presidents.

The Depression undercut Cowen's approach. Pictures and text had conditioned families to see a Lionel train as a necessity in the 1920s. Economic hardship proved it was not. Cowen had no choice but to begin again. Both his company and his dreams needed updating. To start,

The unidentified artist that painted this illustration for the cover of the 1935 catalog couldn't have been more successful in communicating the authority and sophistication of the modernistic design of the Milwaukee Road's *Hiawatha* steam locomotive and Lionel's new O gauge model.

text continues on page 64

The SANTA FE

Above: Lionel raised the bar for postwar trains when it announced replicas of F3 diesels. Santa Fe units, streaking through the Southwest in the 1948 catalog, remained in the line for 18 years, although none was painted black as mistakenly shown.

Below: This image from the 1931 catalog should remove any questions about why certain Standard gauge outfits have become classics. The *Blue Comet* and the Brown State sets have stood the test of time.

nothing better in the line

In every generation there are Lionel trains against which all others are measured. In appearance as well as performance, these items outpace everything else. During the classic era of Standard gauge (1924-33), the "Aristocrats of Miniature Railroading" were the *Blue Comet* and the Brown State sets. Before World War II, when Lionel dedicated its resources to producing accurate O scale models, the New York Central Hudson and Milwaukee Road *Hiawatha* inherited the crown. Ascending next were the Santa Fe F3 diesel and the Pennsylvania GG1. Massive steamers, notably scale models of the Pennsy T1 and the Union Pacific articulated Big Boy, represent the current standard.

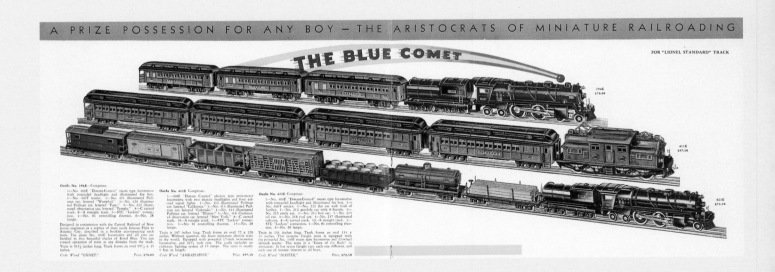

A PRIZE POSSESSION FOR ANY BOY — THE ARISTOCRATS OF MINIATURE RAILROADING

1938

Six superlative O gauge locomotives await their next assignment on the cover of the 1938 catalog. This image, another of the illustrations done by L. Meinrad Mayer, features, among others, the New York Central Hudson, Union Pacific *City of Portland* streamliner, and Milwaukee Road *Hiawatha*. The influence of this illustration lasted into the postwar era, as seen by the cover of the 1952 catalog, which is shown on the dust jacket of this book.

The yards and work shops of the railroads: A water spout to fill the engine's tanks, a turntable for redirecting locomotives and the whole area made bright as day by giant beacon lights.

The watercolors on these two pages, included in a series introduced in the 1935 catalog, capture the romance of Lionel railroading. Toys change into realistic models, and viewers can experience their speed, appreciate their beauty, and feel their authority.

Cowen changed his product line in the mid-1930s. He gradually abandoned Standard gauge because its size, expense, and toylike appearance satisfied fewer consumers. Cowen focused, instead, on a renovated O gauge line split to reach different groups. Low-priced sheet-metal toys occupied one end; expensive, highly accurate models of trains making headlines filled the other.

Lionel artwork reveals how the line changed and sheds light on where Cowen, assisted by Arthur Raphael, his trusted national sales manager, wanted the bifurcated O gauge roster to take his firm. For example, Standard gauge trains did not grace a catalog cover after 1931 (the line survived for eight more years). Instead, after two years of depicting boys with full-sized steam locomotives, a series of spectacular O gauge locomotives greeted readers of the annual wish books. From 1934 on, illustrations in catalogs and ads emphasized the accuracy of new Lionel models

and showed boys and men enjoying the realistic trains together. In style and composition, the pictures reflected Cowen's goals of recapturing the interest of older kids and making trains appealing to men.

Men had in the past been incidental to the Lionel experience. Art had shown them nodding in approval while their offspring played with trains or assuring boys that the models they had bought were like real locomotives and cars. Cowen pushed a different idea, beginning in the mid-1930s. Adults, specifically fathers, should share the joys of operating sets and the challenges of designing and constructing layouts. Pictures depicted two generations of Lionel enthusiasts collaborating in ways that drew them closer and let dads reassert their authority.

Cowen believed that the path-breaking models Lionel developed would do more than fulfill the hopes of sons and fathers. They would also help him achieve his dreams. Just as low-end trains enabled Cowen to reestablish his presence in the toy field, so too would Lionel's scale locomotives and remote-controlled accessories vault him to leadership in the burgeoning adult hobby of scale model railroading. Producing accurate precision models would again raise

Lionel in the public's view and increase its founder's sense of authority.

changes in the line

Recovery from economic despair eventually came for Cowen, his firm, and the country. Sales of electric trains picked up after 1933, which encouraged the president of Lionel to feel hopeful about the future. He saw longtime rivals Hafner and American Flyer shaking off the doldrums, too. Another competitor, Dorfan, stumbled along for a few more years before it succumbed. Ives, Cowen's early nemesis, was already gone, filing for bankruptcy in 1928. At the low end Cowen took on a feisty arrival, Louis Marx, who tried to win sales with cheap windup and electric trains. But Lionel remained king, ruling virtually every niche in the toy train market, even after the A.C. Gilbert Co., maker of the popular Erector set toy, purchased the American Flyer line in 1938.

Lionel concentrated on improving its O gauge offerings. The shift away from Standard gauge, so evident in art from 1934 on, launched a new era in the firm's history. Previously, O gauge trains had occupied a secondary position. This pecking order was reversed as Lionel unveiled the first in a series of outstanding O

gauge models that left the Standard gauge line looking hopelessly out of date. Joseph Bonanno and his crew of design engineers, assisted by the Union Pacific, rushed to finish a model of that railroad's M-10000, a new streamlined train that was taking the country by storm. The unexpected success of this colorful set injected life into the O gauge line.

Rising sales figures for the M-10000 motivated Lionel to cooperate with railroads and locomotive builders to acquire blueprints of the fastest streamliners and flashiest steamers. Between 1935 and 1939, O gauge models of the Milwaukee Road *Hiawatha*, Union Pacific *City of Denver*, and Boston & Maine *Flying Yankee* trains, plus the New York Central and Pennsylania Torpedo steam locomotives, established high standards of excellence. Never before had Lionel manufactured such realistic models, most of which were enhanced by the remote-controlled whistle

You hear the distant whistle of a train, lights flash on at the crossing, bells ring, gates are lowered and a watchman rushes out swinging a lighted lantern.

text continues on page 68

Adding a version of the Union Pacific M-10000 streamliner offered such promise that Lionel broke with tradition and featured O gauge trains on its annual consumer catalog for the first time in 1934. Here, Lionel's "Train of Tomorrow" snakes by a futuristic city for the cover of the September-October 1934 issue of *Lionel Magazine*.

THE LIONEL MAGAZINE

The Model Railroad Magazine for Every Boy

THE LIONEL
"Train of Tomorrow"

IN THIS ISSUE—INTERESTING TRACK LAYOUTS
BUILDING OIL CITY—THE WAR OF THE ROYAL GORGE

# of mice and trains

Fast trains and plucky mice were big news in the 1930s, and Lionel made sure to keep up. Streamlining changed the look of trains as designers, influenced by hydrodynamics and aerodynamics, made them more efficient and attractive by eliminating cracks and sharp lines in favor of smooth contours that reduced air resistance. Lionel developed O gauge versions of the Union Pacific *City of Denver*, the Boston & Maine *Flying Yankee*, and a fictitious streamliner. On a whimsical note, it capitalized on the popularity of Mickey, Minnie, et al., by bringing out a few handcars run by animal power.

Illustrations of the Lionel handcars, especially the model starring Mickey and Minnie Mouse, were as colorful as the animated cartoons drawn at Walt Disney's studio. This image appeared in a 1936 brochure for retailers.

Within the image:

Red Comet

No. 291E "O" Gauge Distant Control Passenger Train

Outfit consists of:
1—No. 264E Distant Control locomotive
1—No. 265T Streamlined coal tender
2—No. 603 Pullman cars
1—No. 604 Observation car

1—No. 88 Reversing controller
1—OC, curved, 2—OS straight track
1—OTC Lockon

The famous Commodore Vanderbilt locomotive hauls the ultra-modern streamlined Red Comet. The vermillion cars have 4-wheel trucks and are 7½ inches long. The entire train is 44½ inches long. Track supplied forms an oval 40 by 30 inches. **Price $10.95**

Type "B" Lionel transformer, of greater capacity, will provide for the addition of many illuminated and automatic accessories. **Price $14.50**

No. 291W Same as No. 291E but with whistle equipment and with No. 66 whistle and reversing controller instead of No. 88.

No. 292E "O" Gauge Distant Control Freight Train

Outfit consists of:
1—No. 264E Distant Control locomotive
1—No. 265T Streamlined coal tender
1—No. 654 Oil tank car
1—No. 652 Gondola car with barrels

1—No. 657 Caboose
1—No. 88 Reversing controller
1—OC, curved, 2—OS straight track
1—OTC Lockon

A crack freight train headed by the powerful, black Commodore Vanderbilt locomotive and tender. Train is 42½ inches long. Track forms an oval 40 by 30 inches. **Price $10.95**

Type "B" Lionel transformer, of greater capacity, will provide for the addition of many illuminated and automatic accessories. **Price $14.50**

No. 292W Same as No. 292E but with whistle equipment and with No. 66 whistle and reversing controller instead of No. 88.

11

Streamliners proved to be such winners that Lionel created its own. The Red Comet, which made its debut in 1936, comes alive in this catalog image, thanks to the bold color and streaking steam in the art.

patented at the same time. Except for running on three-rail track, these train sets were unlike anything from the past.

At the same time that Cowen was forging ahead in his effort to bring out realistic models of the latest equipment and energize the market, he was also struggling to hold on to his traditional audience that just wanted to play with trains. He saw the need to offer less expensive toys whose color and whimsy would make it impossible for parents to deny them to young children. Resources would, as a result, be allocated so Lionel could continue manufacturing the bright sheet-metal models that had been mainstays of the O gauge line since the 1920s.

Most importantly for the millions hungering for a train, Lionel came out with something brand new in 1934 that almost anyone could afford. Capitalizing on the nation's infatuation with Mickey Mouse, it introduced a mechanical handcar featuring characters created by Walt Disney. This low-priced item scooted around a loop of track, thereby proving that you didn't need an entire system to enjoy a Lionel train. Mickey and Minnie, joined by Donald Duck and Santa Claus on other windups, guaranteed joy for families while garnering publicity and revenue for Lionel.

Even though the Disney handcars had zipped out of the catalog by 1938, Lionel went on offering inexpensive sets known as O-27 because they ran on track with tighter curves than O gauge. The O-27 models were a far cry in price, size, and intricacy from the scale Hudson locomotive and streamliners at the top of the line. Some featured lithography, a process Cowen disdained but used because it lowered production costs. Tough times and a combative spirit even drove him to insert windups into the Lionel Jr. line to prevent Marx from stealing the low end of the market.

The windups and lithographed cars at one end of the spectrum and the scale locomotives and remote-controlled freight loaders at the other reveal a line that was probably more segmented than it had been in the 1920s, when Lionel had promoted both O and Standard gauge. Cowen was adamant about reaching every consumer and establishing Lionel as the leader in all fields of miniature railroading. Aware that smaller gauges were gaining popularity, he pressured his engineers to come up with something. They did, and the OO gauge line made its debut in 1938, with a freight set that ran on track whose outer rails were ⅞ inch apart.

new themes in artwork

A range of outstanding illustrations highlighted the innovative O gauge trains and accessories Lionel introduced between 1934 and 1940. This artwork appeared in various places, from catalogs aimed at wholesalers and consumers to ads in mass-circulation magazines and newspapers. What artists depicted and the techniques they employed reinforced certain themes, the most obvious of which was that Lionel currently offered trains unsurpassed in

their realism and performance ("Real Trains in Everything But Size," the 1936 catalog proclaimed). The corollary to this idea was that Lionel would go on augmenting its line with the models that every enthusiast dreamed of.

Just as illustrators had once celebrated the color and size of Standard gauge sets, so in the late 1930s did they strive to capture the realism and sophistication of the Hudson steam locomotive and the *Hiawatha* passenger train. They painted covers that could have doubled as posters for the New York Central or the

text continues on page 72

Showing a young boy wearing a locomotive engineer's garb, as Lionel did for the 1939 catalog, became commonplace only in the 1950s. Late prewar illustrations typically showed older fellows in stylish pullovers and slacks.

1936

LIONEL

L. Meinrad Mayer first shared his talents with Lionel in 1936, when he painted a catalog cover that reflected the firm's commitment to bringing out accurate models of the latest locomotives, including the Pennsylvania Railroad's streamlined Torpedo on the right. He also provided a sneak preview of Lionel's scale New York Central Hudson, which didn't enter the line until 1937.

one artist's realism

From the 1930s into the mid-1950s, L. Meinrad Mayer (1894-1991) enriched Lionel art with covers and catalog designs. A freelance artist trained to paint still-life pictures, his knack for highlighting the precision and detail of new O gauge locomotives meshed perfectly with Lionel's goal in the late prewar era of developing highly realistic scale models. Mayer's influence was also felt after World War II, when his evolving techniques brought out the toylike qualities and pleasures of the new Lionel trains.

Above: Perhaps Mayer's finest achievement at Lionel was the cover of the 1939 catalog. The famed scale New York Central Hudson stands proudly on a brilliant red background, every rivet and valve on display.

Left: Mayer, thanks to his friendship with advertising manager Joseph Hanson, contributed to the design of Lionel publications after World War II. He may have painted the cover for the 1948 consumer catalog, which so nicely blends the realism and toylike whimsy that characterized the trains.

Milwaukee Road. The 1935 catalog hearkened back to Impressionism, with its dazzling hues and imprecise lines. Later covers resembled photographs, with colors true and details sharp.

The streamlined look associated with industrial design and transportation in the prewar era influenced Lionel artwork and printing. Sweeping curves and elongated lettering enlivened different catalog and advertising illustrations, while solid, sans-serif typefaces gave a modern, elegant feel to instruction manuals and the orange-and-blue boxes in which items were packed. Even when there was no doubt that the locomotive or train depicted was a miniature, it still seemed dynamic.

One artist stands out for the great catalog covers he executed. L. Meinrad Mayer began an association with Lionel in the mid-1930s that lasted into the 1950s. During that time he contributed many superb images and likely designed several catalogs, though he preferred to freelance and not accept full-time employment at Lionel. His talents as a painter of portraits and landscapes improved the look of covers between 1936 and 1942. Mayer posed locomotives atop blueprints and amid drafting tools in pictures he could have titled, "Still Life with Electric Train." These scenes reminded viewers of the lengths Lionel had gone to manufacture accurate reproductions.

Besides showing the detail and accuracy of Lionel models, art from the late prewar era explored how trains linked sons and fathers. The Great Depression had threatened and in some cases ripped apart the bonds between generations. Fathers thrown out of work often lost their authority and felt alienated from their children. Boys with unemployed fathers could not be blamed for ignoring the recommendation in the 1932 catalog to "Take your Dad into Partnership." Now, illustrators asserted, those ties could be repaired and families reunited, courtesy of Lionel.

The company's brain trust (Cowen, Raphael, and advertising manager Archer St. John) saw no need to revive the sentimental imagery and flowery language once used to link sons and fathers with a train set. They preferred the somewhat austere approach adopted to highlight the realism of new models and features in the late 1930s. It was enough to show boys and their dads talking about the advantages of Lionel outfits and working together on a layout (both having rolled back the cuffs on their white shirts but not loosened their ties). Artwork, especially the sepia-toned photographs sprinkled throughout the 1940 catalog, left no doubt that the luckiest fellows on earth were the ones with fathers who promised to make Lionel railroading "our hobby."

Newspaper advertisements as well as catalog and magazine illustrations published before and after World War II supported the view that a model railroad was the best way for sons and dads to enjoy each other's company. "Talk to Dad today," advised the 1940 catalog, "Plan together. Work together." Images printed in comic books also emphasized the connections that generations made when they had a train at their disposal. Artists posed an older man touching a boy's shoulder as the two surveyed the sets for sale or their own handiwork because this gesture expressed the reassurance that so many sons longed for: Pop had returned. (What in 1940 meant coming back from economic failure, in 1946 meant coming back from military service.)

Cowen and St. John made certain that the message of trains drawing boys close to their dads influenced the latest incarnation of the firm's magazine. *Model Builder*, the successor to *Lionel Magazine*, first hit newsstands in the spring of 1937. Over the next 12 years, it

trumpeted the benefits in store for any father-and-son team that constructed a Lionel layout. Especially forceful in conveying this notion were the covers. Paintings and color photographs gave way to less costly black-and-white images, but all showed young men happily engaged in building a railroad or operating trains with someone older, presumably their dad.

text continues on page 76

Illustrations such as this, used for the cover of the July-August 1937 issue of *Model Builder*, show the determination of Lionel to become a leader in the hobby world. Building and decorating a structure is the subject of this image; the train in the lower left corner is almost lost.

Above: Lionel Magazine, which ran from 1930 to 1936, was the firm's first regularly published attempt at educating consumers in how much they could do with their trains. Covers, like this one from the January-February 1932 issue, tended to feature well-composed photos rather than paintings.

Right: Hardly skipping a beat, the advertising department replaced *Lionel Magazine* with *Model Builder* in 1937. Original paintings adorned the earliest covers, such as this one from March-April 1937. Was that streamlined locomotive on the boy's turntable something Lionel was planning to build?

creating a hobby

Watching a train chase itself around a loop of track might satisfy a child, but older kids wanted more to do with their trains. To reach these budding model railroaders and boost sales, Lionel produced magazines, books, and pamphlets during the pre- and post-World War II eras. Handsome cover illustrations and photographs distinguished these publications, which offered advice on how to design a layout, build structures, and create scenery so hobbyists could transform their dreams into three-rail masterpieces.

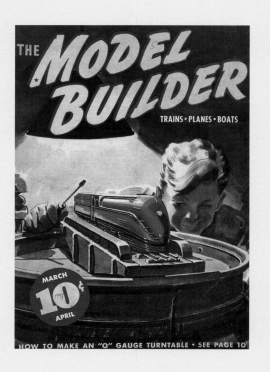

HANDBOOK for MODEL BUILDERS

FUN AND FACTS FOR THE AMATEUR RAILROADER

PRICE FIFTY CENTS

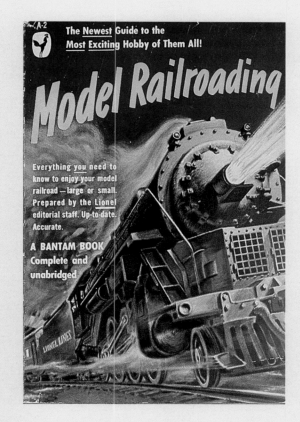

A-2

The Newest Guide to the Most Exciting Hobby of Them All!

Model Railroading

Everything you need to know to enjoy your model railroad—large or small. Prepared by the Lionel editorial staff. Up-to-date. Accurate.

A BANTAM BOOK
Complete and unabridged

Left: Encouraged by the success of *Model Builder* magazine, Lionel put out an anthology of articles as *Handbook for Model Builders* in 1940. The photo on the cover offers a glimpse of the O gauge layout in Lionel's New York showroom.

Above: In 1950, Lionel provided a more comprehensive look at the pleasures and challenges of model railroading. Bantam Books published several editions of this paperback, each having a dramatic cover.

The intertwined themes of Lionel making better, more realistic trains and of fathers and sons strengthening their ties by collaborating on layouts revolved around old-fashioned notions of productivity. During the more prosperous 1920s, when artwork first explored the relationships of electric trains with young men and their dads, it had focused on consumption: fathers buying the best sets and accessories for their sons. A decade later, after enduring economic calamity, people remained wary of spending sprees. Hard work, ingenuity, and thrift once more ranked high among prevailing values, and Cowen preached them as critical to his company and America's families.

Promoting these values bolstered the credibility of Lionel art. Consumers felt they could trust a firm that made excellent products and strove to reunite fathers and sons. The image of Lionel as an authority in its field and a presence in American life gained momentum as the 1930s came to a close. Little did Cowen, Raphael, and others realize how the firm would be tested so soon afterward.

wartime challenges

Less than six months after the Japanese attack on Pearl Harbor plunged the United States into the global war, federal restrictions on the use of "strategic materials" put an end to Lionel's production of electric trains. Even before that catastrophic event in December of 1941, the nation had been upgrading its armed forces, and Lionel had secured contracts to manufacture precision naval instruments. More contracts arrived in subsequent years, so the lights at the company's plant kept burning and its assembly lines never stopped running.

The challenges facing Cowen and his inner circle, which now included his son, Lawrence, were twofold. First, Lionel had to show the public that it had not disappeared but was making vital contributions to the war effort. Second, it had to retain the loyalty of its customers. The latter task involved keeping dedicated model railroaders enthusiastic about Lionel trains when none were available and rallying them to believe that there would soon be even better sets to enjoy in peacetime.

Illustrations played key roles in conveying these messages and helping Lionel remain part of the national consciousness. Even before the country entered the war, catalog images fastened on patriotic motifs to show consumers that Lionel was not caught up in making frivolous luxuries. To this point, Cowen had, by and large, avoided such imagery. Eagles, flags, and red and white stripes had been absent in illustrations, except briefly during World War I. He did not stick "American" in the name of his business, as did one rival, nor scold anyone for not buying trains "Made in U.S.A."

Starting in 1940 and continuing into 1945, however, artwork made certain that consumers associated Lionel with the production of items vital to the country's defense. Pictures in ads and brochures narrated a stirring tale of how the firm had gone from making realistic miniature trains to making precision naval and aeronautical instruments. Artists, especially Louis Melchionne, who joined Lionel in 1942, portrayed this transition as a seamless one. Accuracy and dependability were hallmarks of all Lionel products, regardless of whether they were placed on three-rail track or bolted to submarines and bombers. The implication drawn from wartime illustrations was that lessons learned during the conflict would help Lionel develop better trains when peace returned.

Until then, boys and their dads had to be patient and find ways of maintaining their interest. Cowen turned to artists to prevent his

trains from being forgotten. They filled *Model Builder* with drawings of do-it-yourself projects. Magazine advertisements still carried illustrations, as did comic books and Sunday newspapers. Most important might have been the free booklets loaded with pictures of its trains that Lionel mailed. Like movies and songs, art

text continues on page 80

By the time the *Lionel Railroad Planning Book* came out in 1944, Americans were ready to roll up their sleeves and have fun! They had suffered through the Great Depression and sacrificed for the war effort. Now they looked forward to peace and the chance to enjoy life.

77

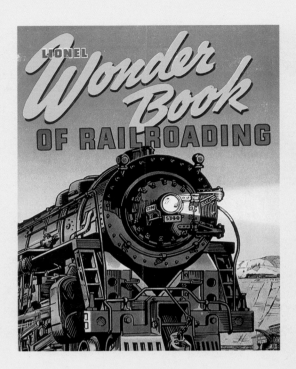

LIONEL GOES TO SEA

Lionel Machinery and Manpower Now Work to Help Win the War

LIONEL'S ABILITY to produce equipment of the finest precision and accuracy has brought contracts from the United States Government for the construction of sensitive Navy instruments relied upon to protect and to guide the course of many units of this nation's great and growing battle fleets.

Illustrated below are a few of the products Lionel is now building to help beat the Axis.

If you have difficulty in locating the Lionel equipment you want for your model railroad, remember that the material and manpower normally devoted to its production is now assigned to help win the war.

Lionel products will be found in many departments of the modern warship. The COMPENSATING BINNACLE (A) holds the ship compass. The PELORUS (B) is a complicated instrument used for obtaining bearings by stellar observation. The ALIDADE (D) is a calibrated sighting device. Lifeboats are equipped with LIFEBOAT BINNACLES (C). As protection against air attacks, warships use anti-aircraft shells (E), which contain Lionel SHELL PRIMERS.

Above right: Even before America's entry into World War II put an end to electric train production, Lionel was manufacturing precision military items. The 1942 catalog reminds youngsters that Lionel, like many of their dads and older brothers, has been drafted. It didn't catalog trains again until 1945.

Above: The *Lionel Wonder Book of Railroading* represented an attempt by Lionel to satisfy its customers in 1943, when the company was not allowed to make electric trains. This booklet shared tips for building layouts and featured black-and-white photographs of real trains. But just as the painting of a scale Hudson on the cover seems flat when compared to prewar cover images, reading about Lionel trains fell short of handling new ones.

Lionel goes to war

By May of 1942, when federal restrictions prohibited using "strategic materials" for toys, Lionel was already proceeding "full speed ahead" with production of compasses, binnacles, and other precision items for the U.S. Navy and Army Air Corps. During the war, it relied on *Model Builder* and a few booklets to keep consumers enthusiastic about electric trains. Articles explained how to plan layouts and to build structures out of wood and cardboard. Those same materials were the foundation of the one train Lionel advertised during the war, the Wartime Freight Train, which proved to be a nightmare to assemble. In 1944, a year after introducing the ill-fated "Paper Train," Lionel brought out a few wood toys for preschool-age children in its Lion-Eds line. Sales were mediocre. All Joshua Cowen and other executives could do as the Allies pushed toward Berlin and Tokyo was wait for permission to resume manufacturing trains and accessories.

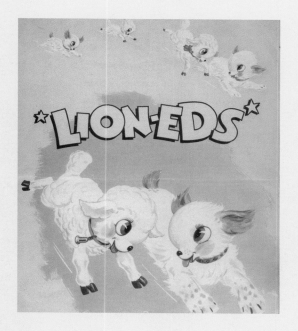

Above: Pictures of navigational instruments and wood playthings in the Lion-Eds line were among the first pieces of art that Louis Melchionne (1907-98) did for Lionel after being hired in 1942. Over the next quarter-century, he designed paint and lettering schemes for freight cars and created dozens of exploded-view drawings for service manuals and instruction sheets.

Opposite below: To satisfy the boys and fathers desperate for a new toy train to enjoy, Lionel issued the Wartime Freight Train for the holiday season of 1943. The cover art makes this cardboard-and-wood set look like fun, but trying to put it together left plenty of kids and parents exasperated.

Inside the advertisement illustration:

"Dreams Coming True"

Boys!—for four years you waited for Lionel Trains, while Lionel was busy helping Uncle Sam win the war! Now Lionel Trains are back again! Gosh!—this is good news, isn't it?

Yes, your dreams are coming true! Wonderful dreams! The new Lionel Trains and accessories are SUPER!

Powerful Locos!—realistic freights and cars!

Thrilling Lionel Trains that you can start and stop, switch about and uncouple by electric REMOTE CONTROL.

Electric magnet-cranes, and coal and lumber cars that you can operate and un-

load at the touch of a button.

Sleek, speedy trains like real trains in everything but size. Boy!—the fun you are going to have!

Of course not everything this year. Limited quantities only at your favorite store. But in 1946—some sensational surprises which we'll tell you about later. (Mail coupon now!)

LIONEL TRAINS AND ACCESSORIES

"Make YOUR dreams come true send this coupon NOW"→

"MODEL BUILDER" MAGAZINE $1.00 YEAR

Eight wonderful issues a year—full of exciting pictures, plans, articles, ideas, and track layouts. Subscribe now! Boys! You need this magazine to help you build more realistic model railroads. Ask any of the thousands of boys who subscribe if it isn't TOPS! Send dollar to Model Builder, 15 East 26th Street, New York 10, New York for your subscription (8 issues).

TWO BIG BOOKS FREE

Exciting books! One called "Candid Camera Shots of Lionel Trains in Action"—the other "Plans and Blue Prints for Model Railroaders". Both FREE!

The Lionel Corporation
Dept. No. C
15 East 26th Street, New York 10, N. Y.
Please rush my Two Big FREE Booklets!

Name_____
Address_____
City_____Zone No.____State_____

NEFF

This illustration masterfully conveys the exuberance felt by youngsters everywhere when they heard that Lionel would be releasing a line of trains after the end of World War II. Wesley Neff (1895-1978) painted it for an ad that appeared in comics sections of newspapers around the country on December 9, 1945.

reminded everyone that someday the fighting would end and a victorious America would again know abundance and security.

When that moment arrived in 1945, illustrations glorified it. Now, comic art declared, Lionel could build electric trains again. Engineers, tool makers, and assemblers once more channeled their energy into bringing out the models that kids loved and families desperately needed to feel safe and secure again.

Artists, meanwhile, seemed to pick up where

they had left off when war ignited and train production was halted. They again relied on highly detailed side views of outfits to show that no one made more realistic models than Lionel did. Images of boys and their fathers working intently on a layout also returned after the war. Art reflected what must have been the overriding concern at Lionel in 1945 and '46. For the firm to reassert its authority, it had to act as though nothing had changed, except that its products were more precise and accurate.

Sensible as this stance was, families wanted something else. Economic collapse and global war had changed the country, and consumers needed more than improved electric trains. The leaders of Lionel soon awakened to this fact, as new models and artwork indicated. Their response, brilliant and forceful, strengthened the firm's reputation and elevated its models into national symbols.

Liberty

NOV. 23, 1946   10c

Book: GRANDFATHER OBJECTS   •   Starting: FOR LOVE OR MONEY
...to almost everything—and little wonder!   Tense thriller by Samuel W. Taylor

Why Americans responded so positively to the scene depicted on the cover of the November 23, 1946 issue of *Liberty* magazine should be obvious. Exhausted from years of economic and military struggle, they were eager to resume the activities of "normal" life, especially spending time with family. Percy Leason (1888-1959), who painted many covers for publications in the United States and Australia, captured the simple pleasure of a father and son resuming a pastime that they had put aside when war erupted. Joseph Hanson, the advertising manager at Lionel, had the latest catalog bound into this issue of *Liberty*, thereby ensuring that millions of people would see the new line and rush to start running trains again.

chapter four
Dreams of security
1946-1964

Neither Lionel's trains nor its illustrations suggested new visions for the company in the years right after World War II. Aside from advertisements in Sunday comics heralding the first new trains in three years, artwork scarcely differed from that seen in the early 1940s. O gauge trains, virtually all of them drab and dark, held prominent places in the line. Realism was the dominant theme, especially now that Lionel had perfected a safe and reliable smoke mechanism for its steam locomotives, including the new Berkshire and Turbine. Catalog covers for 1947 and '48 featured big, powerful trains barreling through urban settings. The heavy, muted style was reminiscent of what L. Meinrad Mayer had done before the war, although his signature was nowhere to be seen.

Most telling were the illustrations that, as before, showed fathers and sons planning model railroads. The men looked middle-aged, too old to have enlisted and fought overseas. The boys were not children eager for their first train set. Facial features and apparel indicated they were on the verge of adolescence. Art suggested that these boys and dads had embarked on Lionel railroading years before and bided their time while war raged and train production was postponed.

Now that Lionel was again permitted to make trains and accessories, they could leave their fantasies behind and, as a father in the 1947 catalog instructed his son, "We'll build it together . . . the finest Lionel Railroad in town!" Dads and their offspring everywhere could at last dust off rolling stock and locomotives, locate tools, and, like Joshua Cowen and his team, resume work.

Thus the central dream at Lionel—rising to prominence in the model railroad hobby—survived the war. Catalog art showed that top executives still thought they could follow

"Which— LIONEL do you want, Son?"

parallel paths to leadership and profitability. One path consisted of O-27 sets for young kids and fathers strapped by an unpredictable postwar economy. The second featured O gauge replicas for serious modelers with more money to spend. Ironically, other than some sheet-metal holdovers in the O-27 roster and a few new engines in the O gauge, the two lines were similar, more so than before the war.

This photograph from the 1946 catalog expresses the dream of boys and men that, after years of depression and war, they could enjoy their trains and gain a sense of security.

dream driving both Joshua and Lawrence Cowen (newly installed as the firm's president) was still to combat the public's temptation to pigeonhole Lionel as a mere toy manufacturer.

Unfortunately for the firm, fighting this old battle served no purpose. Lionel had already lost favor with the adolescents and men making model railroading their hobby. They shunned unrealistic O gauge trains running on three rails, preferring scale replicas, often half the size of Lionel's less-than-perfect pieces, that operated on realistic two-rail track. Dabbling in O gauge represented only a preliminary phase before moving up to more precise models they assembled from scratch or built from kits sold by companies that these enthusiasts praised as the real authorities of the hobby.

The top brass at Lionel did not try to assuage the undercurrent of dissatisfaction with its trains. These men were too savvy to miss seeing that tastes were shifting in one niche. All the same, they minimized its importance. Reviving

Smoke, the latest innovation from Lionel, fills part of the cover of the 1947 catalog. The actual trackside accessories were nowhere near as small and, therefore, correctly proportioned to the Pennsylvania S2 Turbine shown in this painting. Compare this modest Lionel factory with the image from 1917.

For Lionel, however, what mattered was that advances in design and innovations in metal die-casting and plastics molding again enabled it to make the finest, most realistic trains. Catalog images focused on smoking steamers and updated freight cars equipped with operating knuckle couplers. They extolled a miraculous new outfit controlled by radio frequency waves. Advertising art emphasized the fun that fathers and sons could have with sets and accessories that performed so reliably. The

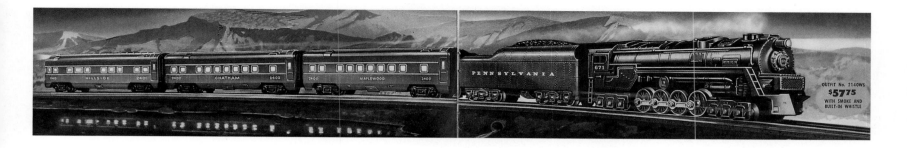

the OO gauge line or entering HO scale, either of which might have placated dedicated hobbyists, wasn't on the agenda after the war. Perhaps Cowen and his associates doubted that they could meet the demands of scale enthusiasts. This might explain why Lionel ceased publication of *Model Builder*, with its construction articles and complex track plans, in early 1949.

Company leaders realized that the market for their trains—and the dreams fueling rising demands—consisted of more than middle-aged men looking for something to do with their sons. Families eager to shape their children into productive citizens and feel secure in an unpredictable world concluded that electric trains were vital to their welfare. Parents bought sets with the same hope that drove their purchases of encyclopedias and savings bonds for their kids. They wanted to prepare the next generation—sons above all—to build a better, safer future. Never before had Lionel models seemed more essential; never since has the public been so enamored of them.

Everyone at Lionel—from the founder of the company to the janitor sweeping up the New York showroom—just stood back and watched in amazement as sales soared year after year. Filling orders taxed the sales staff and exhausted plant supervisors and their employees.

A golden age had arrived at Lionel, thanks to a confluence of factors that no one had predicted and, once there, no one imagined would ever disappear. Artwork of all kinds, from catalog illustrations to drawings in comic books and photographs in magazines, sheds light on how Lionel responded to and sought to direct the social and cultural factors underlying dreams of security.

Above: Mountains painted in soft shades of pink, violet, and blue accentuate the elegant passenger cars and the stolid form of the Pennsylvania Railroad's Turbine in this watercolor in the 1948 catalog.

Left: Headlight beaming and gold stripes shimmering, Lionel's O gauge model of the Pennsylvania Railroad's GG1 electric guides a set of heavyweight passenger cars across this poster, distributed in 1947 and '48. Father and son can't wait to take one home.

Son—let's build the finest Lionel Railroad in town!

Above: What's better, the boy in this illustration from the 1948 catalog might be wondering, to be the owner of Lionel's finest trains and accessories or to have a father eager to spend so much time with him building a layout?

Right: Amid previous covers jammed with trains, the 1949 advance catalog stood out: four silhouettes of the Hudson and tender, each in a different color. That classic locomotive didn't return to the line until 1950.

trains for princes and dads

The first of these factors, an extraordinary pent-up demand for Lionel trains, must have astonished the Cowens. Dreams of a Lionel outfit, delayed for millions of men by national depression and global war, burst forth in the late 1940s, when families at last had a few dollars to spare.

Surprisingly, Lionel all but ignored this new market in its art. Illustrations of sailors or soldiers or even young fathers cradling a Lionel set never appeared. Not even Bernard Relin Associates, the public relations agency that counted Lionel among its accounts, tailored its campaign to highlight the veterans breathless to buy a train. Only in 1949 and continuing for many years after did Lionel acknowledge on its catalog covers that families had become the principal buyers of its trains.

Catalog and advertising artwork reflected a second factor that boosted Lionel's appeal: a fascination with railroading. Publicity about railways

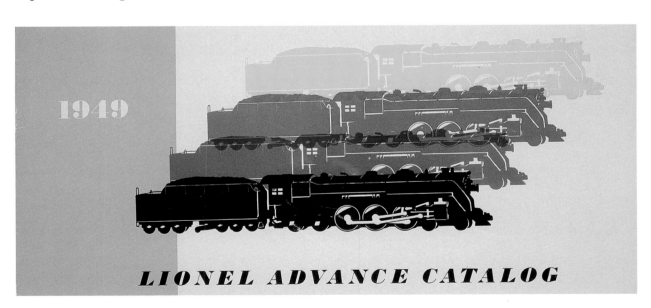

1949

LIONEL ADVANCE CATALOG

OH! BOY!
LIONEL TRAINS
Hear that WHISTLE!—Look at 'em GO! See that Steam Loco puff SMOKE!

expanding services and refurbishing equipment, plus the fact that millions of Americans traveled by train, made this form of transportation part of everyday life. Youngsters counted freight cars, waved to engineers, and occasionally boarded a commuter line or passenger express. Kids, overwhelmed by the size and power of railroads, transferred their interest to the only trains they could dream of controlling. Pictures fed their hunger by showing Lionel sets racing across valleys and through cities.

Illustrations capitalized on the nation's interest by linking Lionel models to well-known trains, as had been done in the 1930s. Fanfare surrounded the release of O gauge versions of the Pennsylvania Railroad's GG1 electric-profile locomotive and the Santa Fe's F3 diesel in 1947 and '48, respectively. A picture in the catalog for 1951 depicted a father telling his son and daughter that Lionel's "big, powerful, super-detailed" steam and diesel locomotives were "Miniature masterpieces of perfection,

Boys! Build a real Railroad with **LIONEL TRAINS** ... we'll show you how!

Nothing beat a Lionel train. Marching in a parade, scoring the winning touchdown, and seeing a big league ballgame came close, but for boys like the two shown in this advertisement from the November 20, 1949, *Washington Sunday Star*, there was no greater pleasure than owning an electric train set, especially if it was led by Lionel's new Santa Fe F3.

both in appearance and in operation." Because the posters Lionel mailed to department stores and toy shops were so large and colorful, they best expressed the feeling that owning one of these models was almost as good as sitting in the cab with the engineer.

Nothing a boy could receive was as sophisticated and magical as an electric train. The emotions he felt on opening his first Lionel set—of being mature, trustworthy, and capable—made it almost a rite of passage. "Men of Tomorrow choose Lionel Today," declared the 1952 catalog.

Grandfathers and fathers had felt the same way. Tradition pushed them to buy Junior a Lionel set; knowledge of what Junior's pals already had incited him to beg for one.

Yet even these different factors do not completely explain the fervor for Lionel that was felt across the country for more than a decade after the war. To gain a full understanding, artwork proves critical. Illustrations reflected and promoted two social and cultural phenomena that made buying an electric train (and for most people that meant a Lionel) an absolute necessity.

Not long after Germany and Japan had surrendered, Americans sensed that their yearning for serenity was nowhere near being met. Economic uncertainties and international tensions made security as elusive as ever. Searching for ways to alleviate their nervousness about current conditions and fears of the future, members of the upper and middle classes turned to consumption. They purchased automobiles, houses, appliances, and furniture.

For their children—and the numbers of youngsters were skyrocketing thanks to what's known as the "baby boom"—families in every economic level bought toys. Dolls, stuffed animals, bicycles, cowboy suits, miniature ovens, roller skates, pedal cars, nurse's kits, construction sets, cap pistols, puppets, and jump ropes filled wish lists. At the top for most boys, as well as a few girls, was an electric train.

Interlaced with a deep longing for security was the belief that creating a better, happier future depended on rearing a better, happier generation of boys. Educators and other "children's experts" advised parents to give tomorrow's men what they needed to feel a sense of mastery and to understand the society they would one day shape. The best toys expanded a boy's knowledge and raised his confidence that he could contribute to a prosperous, secure world.

Few playthings met these criteria more fully than did an electric train. To bolster a sense of security while helping develop a generation of enlightened leaders, families turned once more to Lionel. They weren't asking that it serve as the authority in a hobby that seemed too serious for most people. Instead, at a time when Americans dreamed of being able to look to the future with calm and assurance, they wanted Lionel to once more provide toys. Parents needed playthings that brought fun and laughter to children while teaching their sons (catalogs kept referring to them as "young engineers") about modern life and filling them with a sense of efficacy.

Lionel art captured these needs, anxieties, and dreams in the late 1940s and early '50s. Of

Bright eyes, gleaming smiles, and Dad's strong embrace convey a sense of security and happiness in this advertisement from the *Detroit Free Press* of November 23, 1951.

text continues on page 92

"Neato!" "Slick!" "Swell!" Those are the words about to pop out of the mouths of these boys once they see what their buddy has in his basement. This wonderland of American Flyer trains and Erector set models filled the cover of the A.C. Gilbert Co.'s 1950 catalog.

different work at Gilbert

Boys who came of age in the postwar era never quit arguing about whether Lionel trains looked as realistic and ran as smoothly as those made by its major rival, the A.C. Gilbert Co. That firm, known for its Erector sets and Mysto-Magic kits, entered the toy train arena in 1938, when it purchased the American Flyer Manufacturing Co.'s line. After the war, Gilbert redesigned its trains to run on S gauge two-rail track, which was narrower than Lionel O gauge three-rail track. Gilbert's art, handsome in its own right, took an approach different from Lionel's when promoting electric trains. Boys tended to be the only people shown in catalog illustrations or magazine advertisements. Gilbert never capitalized on the notion that its American Flyer trains might strengthen the bonds uniting members of families, especially fathers and sons.

Top: Lionel emphasized the pleasure entire families, rather than just boys, had with its trains. In 1951, it showed a mother on the front cover of its catalog and a younger sister in this picture from the rear cover. Still, a closer look suggests that the trains are for Dad and Junior; about all that Sis will get to do is smell the smoke.

Above: In 1952, the cover of the American Flyer catalog featured only trains and toys as elements in a technological paradise. Banning Repplier, a former Lionel employee, handled advertising for Gilbert in the 1950s. He aimed the art at children rather than families.

archetypal American family: father and mother, their son, and his younger sister. These images, which graced consumer catalogs and magazine advertisements, reflected the wish that trains would unite families and not enable sons and fathers to escape. To be sure, the latter concept survived in ads in comic books and Sunday comics sections, media aimed directly at boys. But where women were likely to come across advertisements, Lionel pushed the idea that everyone would be having fun with its trains.

The most sentimental of Lionel's postwar illustrations enhanced a series of advertisements that appeared in some of the country's favorite magazines between 1949 and 1954.

Above: Pop looks as excited as his son is about their eye-opening roster of Lionel trains. This ad from the *Detroit News* of November 16, 1953, makes you wonder how long Junior will be permitted to stay at the controls.

importance were the illustrations and photographs that, for the first time, depicted the

Right: Life was never sweeter for a boy than when he received a Lionel freight or passenger outfit equipped with Magne-Traction. Even a fellow as young as the one in the center of this store poster released in 1953 knew he had climbed to the top of the three-rail mountain.

Joseph Hanson, who served as advertising manager at Lionel from 1945 through 1955, deserves credit for commissioning these wonderful images. Already, he had masterminded the move that put a painting of a Lionel set by Percy Leason on the cover of *Liberty* magazine in 1946 and stapled a copy of the consumer catalog inside. Hanson had taken this daring step when a nationwide paper shortage threatened to restrict distribution of the Lionel catalog and so weaken sales.

Whereas the cover of *Liberty* featured a father and son, the pictures in *Life*, *Collier's*, and *Saturday Evening Post* in the early 1950s tended to show families. The son was the centerpiece, younger than his counterpart in *Liberty* and no longer just a partner of his father. Instead, the train was his to run. The boy kept a hand on the transformer and guarded the track. Mom and Dad sat back and watched with a smile. Little sister did her best to catch a glimpse of what was happening. Yet as was customary in Lionel art, she was expected to stay out of the way.

Other illustrations omitted parents and siblings to concentrate on the boy dreaming of a train. By depicting a boy blissfully envisioning what he might receive for Christmas, artists

underscored the message that a Lionel train was for him and him alone. Typically, they portrayed youngsters dressed in pullover shirts and blue jeans. These young princes had curly blond hair, ruddy cheeks, and bright eyes, traits parents easily recognized as similar to those of their own slightly mischievous yet sweet "angels" wishing

text continues on page 96

The peace of mind that families could find at home with a Lionel set was expressed in this ad from the November 16, 1953, *Saturday Evening Post*. In an uncertain world, parents and kids feel safe within the circle of track.

baby boomers dream

People couldn't got enough of Lionel after World War II. Its trains were as popular as Milton Berle or General Eisenhower, thanks in part to the full-color advertisements found in such mass-circulation magazines as *Life, Saturday Evening Post, Collier's, Esquire,* and *National Geographic.* These sentimental pictures tended to show young boys, by themselves or with their families, dreaming of the wonderful trains they might receive if they were good. Their smiles, like the array of train sets, grew larger every year.

Above: The image in the November 22, 1952, *Saturday Evening Post* captures the marvelous aspect of Lionel trains. Outfits that consist of only a few cars stretch into the distance until each is a blur of color. So too a child's imagination transforms a set into something as grand as the longest and fastest express on the Baltimore & Ohio or the Southern Pacific.

Right: Boys weren't the only ones spellbound by a Lionel train. Fathers exhausted after a day spent pushing wheelbarrows or pencils needed to play. Uncoupling cars and blowing a steamer's whistle provided that relief, as shown in this ad in the November 1953 *Hunting & Fishing* magazine.

A ONE-TRACK MIND !

When it comes to trains, boys have a one-track mind.
They want Lionel Trains...nothing else is the real thing. They
know that only Lionel has *Magne-Traction.**
They know that nothing else approaches the true-to-life realism
of Lionel's scale detailing. You can't fool today's youngsters...
and for solid value, it's better not to try. Just follow
his "one-track mind" to your Lionel dealer's!

**The permanent power-plus that means . . .*
More Speed! More Pull! More Climb! More Control!

LIONEL TRAINS

LIONEL

Stop in at your Lionel dealer's for the great new 40-page Lionel Trains catalog

Electric trains filled the dreams of boys in the 1950s, maybe even more than a baseball glove or a bicycle did. They told the world, the hero of this advertisement would agree, that a kid was growing up. He was ready to drop smoke pellets into the stack of a steam locomotive, unload miniature milk cans and logs, and build a layout with his dad. Alex Ross (1909-90), whose watercolors were used for the covers of *Good Housekeeping, Collier's, Ladies' Home Journal,* and *Cosmopolitan*, painted this illustration in the November 16, 1953, *Life* magazine. It captures what electric trains meant to a generation of children after World War II.

artists urged parents to let their offspring play innocently now. The underlying notion was that the world these boys would enter and strive to control was uncertain and dangerous. Decent, industrious men at times fell short of success. Even the men who did manage to climb the ladder could lose touch with their loved ones and their past. Security might not be possible, even for kids who grew up with Lionel, so please let them play in peace.

Artists did hold out hope, though. They offered an antidote to the routines of business that robbed a man of his enthusiasm and independence and left him a virtual stranger to his wife and children. Getting back on the floor to play again with a Lionel electric train set could save him. The sober demeanor and distance

Lionel all but promised in this Sunday comic, which ran on November 21, 1954, that owning a train set guaranteed that lonely "fellas" would never again be left out of the good times.

for a new locomotive or freight loader. What parent could be so cold-hearted or shortsighted as to refuse to buy a Lionel set for such a lad?

As the years passed, the boys in these illustrations seemed younger and more childlike. Their creators put forward a second, somewhat contradictory message. Without denying that a Lionel set ably prepared kids for the adult world,

Left: For boys after World War II, no toy was as sophisticated and demanded as much responsibility as an electric train. The thrill of receiving a new Lionel set is evident from the expressions depicted on the cover of the 1954 catalog.

Below: This ad from the November 15, 1954, *Saturday Evening Post* captures the "paternal bargain." Fathers gave their sons Lionel trains to prepare them for adulthood; by inviting Dad to play, a boy rescued him from the ill effects of the business world.

expected of fathers before the war (seen even in Lionel artwork) should be banished. "Pop" needed to stay close to his sons while remaining jovial, a true "boy at heart."

The men in gray flannel suits resisted putting down their newspapers to recall the joys of a train. That's where, according to illustrators, sons were critical. Boys had to rescue their dads from the world of labor and commerce that, ironically, a Lionel set was preparing them to join. They did so, as Raymond Crowley in particular liked to show, by emulating dads in dress

and mannerisms as a ploy to coax them onto the floor. Once there, fathers relaxed and then eagerly grabbed the transformer.

By 1954, the last year Lionel paid for these full-page color advertisements in large-format magazines, artwork was showing what might be termed the "paternal bargain" behind every Lionel set. In a world beset by insecurity, fathers should make a purchase

Lionel seemed to introduce impressive sets, accessories, and locomotives every year. One of the highlights of 1954 was the lash-up of Southern Railway F3 diesels shown charging over a viaduct in this catalog image.

as important to their sons' well-being and future success as orthodontic braces. They must buy an electric train so that their sons could first experience the wonders and pleasures of a set and then, once old enough, gain familiarity with the roles and demands expected of them as adults. Dads who neglected this responsibility jeopardized their sons' future and risked losing the love and respect of their offspring.

Sons, however, had an equally vital task, according to Lionel art. Because the business world endangered men and pulled them away from families, boys must insist that their fathers join in the fun. Let a Lionel train remind dads of what it was like to be young and innocent.

Pictures of happy boys and men were accompanied by admonitions to women to buy a Lionel set "for those boys of yours." Other images alluded to the troubles caused when families did not buy a train. Kids felt excluded and lost, their ties with peers and mentors torn and their prospects compromised.

Illustrations emphasized that, for sons and fathers in the 1950s, Lionel trains were the keys to a satisfying life. More than ever before, locomotives, sets, and accessories were presented as enjoyable and educational. They guaranteed youthful pleasures now and instilled feelings of mastery and habits of industry and thrift for tomorrow. They delighted kids, trained boys, and saved men, all the while tightening family ties in a world rocked by tension and unease.

Artwork enhanced the appeal of Lionel trains because it connected them to contemporary dreams and the hopes of families. Perhaps that's why Lionel saw no need to include celebrities in its illustrations or follow new fads. Sports heroes, movie stars, and cartoon characters, used to promote a variety of consumer goods in the postwar years, hardly ever appeared in Lionel's advertising. Tiny portraits of Joe DiMaggio, the baseball immortal and Lionel enthusiast, appeared in 1950 only because he had a role on a television series the company sponsored. The ads that Hanson placed in 3-D comic books when that craze hit the United States in 1953 likely represented favors to his predecessor, Archer St. John, who was then struggling to stay afloat as a publisher of some of these periodicals.

Otherwise, Lionel art ignored the fads and stars of the immediate postwar years: Hopalong Cassidy, Captain Marvel, the Lone Ranger, and Howdy Doody—not one of them was linked with Lionel. (Superman did help a rival in the late 1940s by inviting boys to visit the Gilbert Hall of Science and see the American Flyer line.) Lionel believed that emphasizing the superiority of its trains and connecting them with families and dreams of security would suffice. By and large, this proved correct.

balanced lineup

Americans put their trust in Lionel trains and transformed them into icons. Changes in the trains themselves facilitated this process. From the undersized, nondescript models introduced after the war, Lionel went to a lineup character-

ized by color and variety in the mid-1950s. New engines, improved freight cars, and elegant passenger outfits revived the catalog. These items constituted a line that balanced the finest traits of toys with the precision and reliability of sophisticated replicas. A golden age reminiscent of the classic era of Standard gauge emerged between 1952 and 1958.

Anyone who grew up at that time with a Lionel set can recall the beauty, heft, and power that combined to deliver so much fun and excitement. Leafing through catalogs from the 1950s will have to do for anyone younger. Fortunately, the illustrations of graceful F3s, massive Train Masters and Geeps, and sleek EP-5 electrics convey the magic of Lionel's locomotives. Those units, as well as die-cast

Lionelville, every square inch loaded with animation and industry, never looked more impressive than it did in this painting in the 1952 catalog. The array of accessories attested to the ingenuity of the firm's engineers.

text continues on page 102

the greatest year

Above: Artists made excellent use of the space at their disposal on each two-page spread in the 1954 catalog. They featured only a pair of sets, such as these two F3 freight outfits, and developed scenery sure to fascinate and heighten the appeal of these outstanding trains.

Right: The stunning no. 2245 *Texas Special* F3 A-B combination, resplendent in red and white, brought a bit of swagger, typical of the Lone Star State, to the Lionel line in 1954.

Innovation and variety explain why so many collectors of postwar trains believe the Lionel line for 1954 was the finest of the era. Color was another key element. Not since the heyday of Standard gauge had catalog artists been so free to experiment with shades of blue, red, green, and orange. Even better, advertising and sales executives let them take advantage of the space available and encouraged them to place sets in scenes whose detail and texture complemented the beauty of the trains and enhanced their size and realism.

The mammoth and rugged no. 2321 Lackawanna Train Master, another distinguished member of the Class of '54 at Lionel, barely breaks a sweat pulling a train that stretches far into the distance in this illustration on the cover of the 1954 advance catalog.

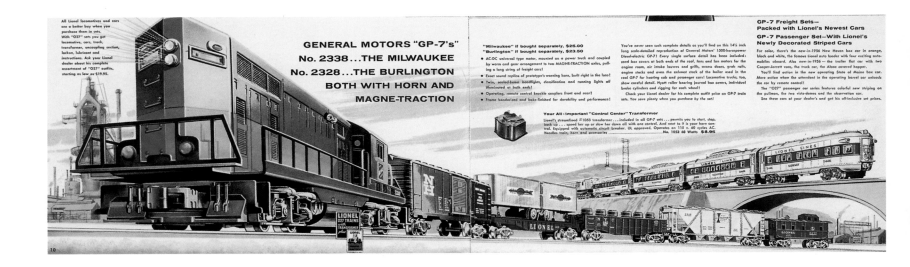

GENERAL MOTORS "GP-7's"
No. 2338...THE MILWAUKEE
No. 2328...THE BURLINGTON
BOTH WITH HORN AND
MAGNE-TRACTION

"Milwaukee" if bought separately, $25.00
"Burlington" if bought separately, $23.50

• AC-DC universal type motor, mounted on a power truck and coupled by worm and gear arrangement to two MAGNE-TRACTION axles, pulling a long string of freight cars!
• Exact sound replica of prototype's warning horn, built right in the loco!
• Twin, sealed-beam headlights, classification and running lights all illuminated at both ends!
• Operating, remote control knuckle couplers front and rear!
• Frame bonderized and bake-finished for durability and performance!

You've never seen such complete details as you'll find on this 14½ inch long scale-detailed reproduction of General Motors' 1500-horsepower Diesel-electric GP-7! Every single surface detail has been included: sand box covers at both ends of the roof, fans and fan motors for the engine room, air intake louvres and grills, access doors, grab rails, engine stacks and even the exhaust stack of the boiler used in the real GP-7 for heating cab and passenger cars! Locomotive trucks, too, show careful detail. Hyatt roller bearing journal box covers, individual brake cylinders and rigging for each wheel!

Check your Lionel dealer for his complete outfit price on GP-7 train sets. You save plenty when you purchase by the set!

GP-7 Freight Sets—
Packed with Lionel's Newest Cars
GP-7 Passenger Set—With Lionel's
Newly Decorated Striped Cars

For color, there's the new-in-1956 New Haven box car in orange, black and white, the famous Lionel auto loader with four exciting automobiles aboard. Also new-in-1956 — the trailer flat car with two Cooper-Jarrett vans, the truck car, the Alcoa covered hopper.

You'll find action in the new operating State of Maine box car. More action when the attendant in the operating barrel car unloads the car by remote control!

The "O27" passenger car series features colorful new striping on the pullman, the two vista-domes and the observation car.

See these cars at your dealer's and get his all-inclusive set prices.

Your All-Important "Control Center" Transformer

Lionel's streamlined #1053 transformer... included in all GP-7 sets... permits you to start, stop, back up... speed her up or slow her down all with one control. And next to it is your horn control. Equipped with automatic circuit breaker. UL approved. Operates on 115 v. 60 cycles AC. Handles train, horn and accessories .... No. 1053 60 Watts $8.95

We feel dwarfed by the Milwaukee Road GP7 road diesel bearing down on us and about to leap off this page. The artist's techniques let readers of the 1956 catalog sense the beauty and power of this locomotive and that of the New Haven EP-5 electric on the next page. The expensive offset printing and the glossy, text (70-pound) paper that Lionel used, gave the catalog greater elegance.

metal steamers, pulled a growing roster of near-scale freight cars decorated for railroads from every region, along with gleaming aluminum streamliners and handsome plastic coaches.

The impetus for Lionel to refurbish its O gauge line in the mid-1950s came from outside corporate headquarters. America's railroads blazed the trail by decking out diesels in flashy colors and introducing a range of new equipment. They wanted their trains to stand out and entice more travelers and shippers. Kids certainly paid attention to these changes. Soon they were clamoring for models that looked as gorgeous as what they saw on the Santa Fe, Wabash, Southern, and other railroads. But Lionel seemed to be the last to notice. The powers-that-be let a couple of rivals get the jump on them. The A.C. Gilbert Co., which

had revamped its American Flyer brand after the war, brought out a complete system of trains, track, and accessories. American Model Toys posed less of a threat, although its streamliners and near-scale boxcars had an immediate impact on Lionel.

Changes on American railroads and heightened competition in the toy train field lit a fire under Lionel. To maintain leadership it dispensed with the prewar holdovers, small boxcars, black operating cars, and drab locomotives that filled its roster after the war. Fortunately for its reputation, Lionel could offer green F3s, blue-and-white boxcars, and yellow stockcars and still proclaim its trains to be paragons of accuracy. It achieved a near-perfect balance of the fanciful and realistic because full-sized trains resembled giant toys. Had Lionel waited

much longer or tried to please adult hobbyists with replicas of older equipment, it might have lost its throne, deposed by upstarts.

Lionel delivered those models, not to mention ingenious operating cars and accessories, in the 1950s. Memorable catalog art revealed the beauty and wonder of these trains. The illustrations of that time stood out as much as the trains did, probably because artists, like the company's engineers, were given free rein to allow their imaginations to soar.

Consider the magnificent two-page views of sets amid landscapes. These broke with tradition. For one thing, pictures of outfits rarely stretched over both pages during the prewar era. Even when artists began using entire spreads after the war, they typically painted trains iden-

tical in size and detail resting on parallel tracks and blocked out against plain backgrounds. Everything seemed cramped, small, and dull. Any sense of motion vanished.

Illustrators started departing from these conventions in the late 1940s. On occasion, they used watercolors (principally blues, magentas, and yellows) to create warm and hazy backgrounds against which top-of-the-line trains were shown. Posing sharply drawn locomotives and cars in front of soft skies and blurred landscapes suggested speed and animation. By the 1950s, artists were depicting fewer sets on individual spreads and varying the angles. They positioned trains lower on the pages and turned one so it seemed about to dash off the spread. Sometimes they deliberately distorted the

perspective, so a locomotive filled much of one page while the cars it pulled shrank rapidly. All of these tricks made outfits seem bigger, more realistic, and more alive.

The art only improved as the years passed. Illustrators took even greater advantage of the horizontal format of Lionel catalogs. They used a variety of techniques (pens, brushes, and air-brushes) and media (India ink, watercolors, and tempera paints) to portray outfits driving through a range of rural, urban, and industrial scenes. Sometimes trains crossed over one another on bridges and trestles. At others, one veered off toward a station or yard, leaving its companion to pass an oil field, desert mesa, or cattle ranch. The effect was spectacular, and these images must have fueled a million dreams

of youngsters intent on building the finest Lionel layout in town.

By relying on the pastels and warm tones in their palettes, illustrators captured the beauty of the bright diesels and freight cars that Lionel was producing. They applied their paints smoothly and allowed lines to flow so nothing jarred viewers. They bathed models in light to accentuate details and curves.

Robert Sherman, the most well-known of Lionel's postwar artists, used techniques intended to make locomotives seem more sub-stantial and sets more impressive. He designed illustrations and prepared black-and-white sketches upon which professionals at agencies splashed on color. Sherman posed models so viewers observed them from three-quarter

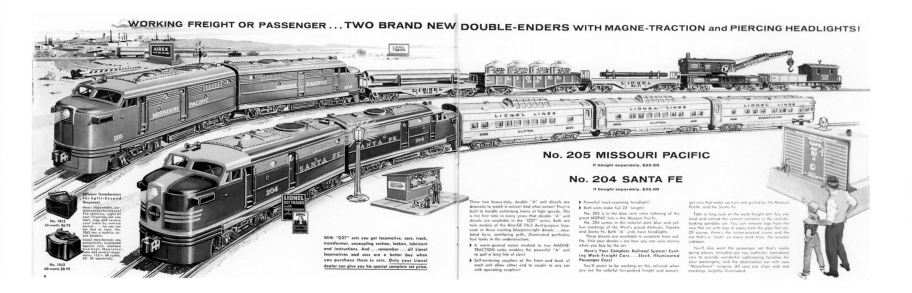

WORKING FREIGHT OR PASSENGER...TWO BRAND NEW DOUBLE-ENDERS WITH MAGNE-TRACTION and PIERCING HEADLIGHTS!

No. 205 MISSOURI PACIFIC
If bought separately, $22.50

No. 204 SANTA FE
If bought separately, $25.00

angles. That technique, like the practice of showing trains as though one were looking up at them, made their features stand out so that everything appeared larger and more inspiring.

A skilled modeler and designer of track plans for *Model Builder* magazine, Sherman understood that trains looked better when set in a landscape. He helped pioneer a concept that raised Lionel art to a peak in the 1950s. Sherman and other artists portrayed sets in a range of scenes, so that flipping through a catalog was like unfolding a pile of travel brochures. Brawny work trains roared by steel mills and along docks in illustrations. Elegant streamliners glided along forested hills and by placid lakes. Hustling freights accelerated past green farms, snowy mountains, and busy cities. Coal

loaders, signal bridges, gang cars, and switch towers dominated railroad yards and terminals.

These catalog images, like the trains they showed, neatly balanced realism with whimsy. The settings resembled those seen in picture postcards: the colors were perfect, and everything was in place. The train was key, with other elements drawing out its beauty and authority. Artists strove to portray models and sets faithfully, yet still took liberties to accentuate the speed and grandeur of Lionel trains.

These illustrations lacked the precision or clarity of a photograph, but an exact view would have spoiled the effect. For merchants who needed to know what a train looked like, Lionel jammed black-and-white snapshots in its advance catalogs. But advertising executives and

Tighter advertising budgets caused catalog illustrations to decline a bit in quality during the late 1950s. Minimal scenery and formulaic compositions eroded the aura of realism and left Lionel trains, like these small Alco diesels in the 1957 catalog, looking more like toys.

text continues on page 110

105

Dockside tracks lead freight loads straight to waiting ships. Loads from some cars are transferred by 24 crane to the holds of waiting ships. Other cars are loaded onto barges (see the slip with tracks leading to water's edge in center) or hoisted onto huge ships called sea trains.

Above: The illustrations Robert Sherman executed for *The Golden Book of Trains* in 1954 taught youngsters how railroads operated. He used Lionel models as the basis of his artwork.

Right: The smooth lines, exaggerated details, and flowing colors that became trademarks of Sherman's work distinguish this part of the 1951 catalog. He made viewers feel the dynamism and life of Lionel trains.

Sherman's trains

Lionel postwar art, and the memories of so many baby boomers, would not be the same without Robert Sherman (1912-95). This fine artist and accomplished model maker proved how depictions of trains could increase the pleasures of model railroading. Sherman's influence would have been great if his only work for Lionel had been the track plans he did for *Model Builder* before World War II and the dioramas he built to be photographed for catalogs and brochures after the war. Yet he had a more lasting impact, thanks to the renderings of outfits he inked for catalogs and the crisp, accurate technical illustrations he created for other Lionel publications.

Sherman was as much a master using three
dimensions to capture the joy of Lionel trains as
he was with two. After World War II, he built
dioramas that, when photographed by his
friend William Vollheim, were used by the
advertising department in promotional materials.

Above: The delight that family members took in running a Lionel train at Christmas comes out in this work by Raymond "Ralph" Crowley. His belief that Dad should have as much fun as Junior comes out in this ad from the November 1951 *National Geographic*.

Right: Dad follows while his son rushes to a store window to admire a great new Lionel outfit in this Crowley illustration, which was used for the cover of the 1960 advance catalog. Seeing the two "men" dressed alike suggests that they'll be equal partners in building a layout, an activity that will strengthen their bonds.

Crowley's families

Just as Robert Sherman illustrated the trains we remember from the 1950s, Raymond Crowley (1898-1972) painted the people. Crowley's training in Chicago and New York had led to a lucrative career as a magazine illustrator by the time former advertising manager Jacques Zuccaire recruited him to depict the happy families using Lionel trains. Bright eyes and grins characterized the boys Crowley painted. Their dads were no less fascinated with the new trains. Maybe that was the secret behind Crowley's success: He understood how toy trains connected fathers and sons by enabling grown men to act like youngsters again.

The kids may be showing excitement as they anticipate their first Lionel train, but it's Dad who is the center of attention in this illustration used as the cover of a promotional catalog for retailers in 1956. Crowley saw no reason that fathers had to turn over control to their sons, not when operating a streamliner was the reward for bringing home the bacon.

From space-age trains and military accessories to old-time steam locomotives of all vintages, the wrap-around cover of the 1959 catalog featured a little of everything. Even Airex, a Lionel subsidiary that sold fishing equipment and sporting goods, received attention.

artists knew that youngsters and parents wanted their imaginations piqued. To that end, Hanson and his successor, Jacques Zuccaire, filled the annual wish books with vivid, majestic artwork.

different form of security

Sadly for Lionel, its balanced line and superb illustrations could no more guarantee perpetual profits than they could ensure feelings of security for every young consumer. Time marched on, and the confluence of factors that made an electric train the ideal gift for a boy ceased to exist. Organized athletics and hot rods, both emblems of growing up, distracted Lionel operators and left them believing that trains were for little kids and not guys dreaming of a letterman's jacket or a Chevy Bel-Air.

Lionel executives, worried that their market was slipping away, even reached out to little girls. They developed a specially decorated set in 1957 that was known as the Lady Lionel. But their effort was only half-hearted, to judge from the minimal advertising done to promote this pastel train and the lackluster illustration of the outfit buried inside the catalog. After appealing strictly to boys for so long, company leaders had no idea how to reach girls.

Of course, by the late 1950s there weren't many kids, male or female, who still took seriously the idea that an electric train might prepare them for adulthood. They were too busy struggling to escape from their parents' control. The cultural and social circumstances that had made Lionel a household name and helped its sales boom had evolved. The diminishing importance of Lionel coincided with the decline of American railroads now that more people were traveling by commercial airliners or via superhighways. Furthermore, trains lacked the excitement of jet planes, so boys idolized test pilots rather than locomotive engineers.

Lionel fought back by focusing on the quest for a different sort of security. With Americans worried about global rivalries, military trains seemed the best way to boost sales. Now, missile-launching vehicles traversed O gauge track. Exploding boxcars, flatcars carrying helicopters and satellites, and Marine Corps cabooses joined them. Rocket launchers and ammo dumps, along with other space and military accessories, replaced coal ramps, log loaders, and icing depots. Young engineers would again feel secure and appreciate their Lionel trains as they fired shots at nameless enemies

and attacked invaders from distant planets.

Catalog illustrations tried to convey the thrills of the new military and space items. Lionel depended on this art because it no longer ran full-page ads in mass-circulation magazines, Sunday supplements, and comic books. Tight budgets in the late 1950s and early '60s meant that catalogs featured fewer, lower-quality illustrations. Images of trains weren't as sharp or realistic as before. Too often sets looked like juvenile playthings and not sophisticated replicas.

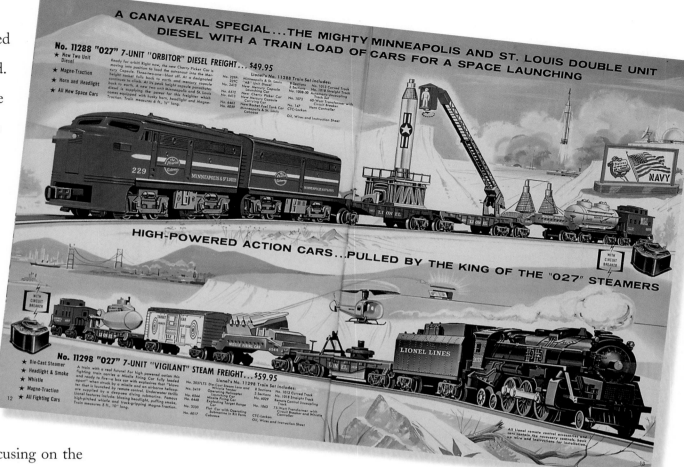

Novel sets, freight cars, and accessories appeared in the late 1950s and early '60s. As seen in the 1962 catalog, Lionel hoped to tap into the public's concern with military security and passion for space exploration.

ANNUAL REPORT

The LIONEL CORPORATION

Year Ended February 28, 1950

The postwar dream of security and prosperity came to life in this wonderful image used for the Lionel annual report of 1950. Mom has a strand of pearls, Dad's got his books, and Sonny's running a Santa Fe set. Best of all, as Little Sis might exclaim, "We're together!" What more could any of them want?

Instead of trains racing by ranches or through deserts, catalogs returned to plopping different models on adjacent tracks to show the breadth of the latest lineup. Creativity seemed to disappear, replaced by only a wish to pose lots of trains and hope that something proved interesting.

Artwork that might have been used in a recruiting pamphlet inspired few dreams. Boys sought a sense of security elsewhere, much as they turned from electric trains to a host of new toys or sporting goods for enjoyment. Lionel, which had used art to express its concern for families and their sons, adopted a different vision under a new group of leaders in the early 1960s.

The two Cowens left, taking with them the firm conviction that tradition, innovation, and craftsmanship would persuade consumers that Lionel was more than just a toy maker. Worn out and dispirited by the financial decline of the company he had founded, Joshua sold control in 1959. Lawrence hung on into the next year until he realized that his influence had disappeared.

Standing at the helm now was Joshua Cowen's grand-nephew Roy Cohn, who had already made a name for himself aiding Senator Joseph McCarthy in the hunt for Communists. Cohn demanded that Lionel improve its earnings and inflate the value of its stock. Determined to find a magic bullet, he expanded the product line to include racing cars, science kits, juvenile phonographs, and commercial aeronautic and military devices, in addition to trains. The only security that mattered anymore was Lionel's.

LIONEL TRAINS

1962

and ACCESSORIES

THE LEADER IN MODEL RAILROADING

"027" SUPER "O" HO

American families never stopped yearning for security and stability in the postwar era. By the time Lionel released its 1962 catalog, that longing increasingly focused on protection from external threats. Now the familiar theme of a son commanding his trains included firing missiles and blowing up special boxcars.

chapter five
Dreams of nostalgia
1963-1993

Change was definitely afoot at Lionel in the early 1960s, as Roy Cohn supervised a mighty expansion of the firm's product line. Worried that trains were losing popularity, his cohorts pushed Lionel into the area of "educational toys." They believed (incorrectly, as it turned out) that the best way for the company to thrive was to imitate the A.C. Gilbert Co., itself barely hanging on. Catalogs soon bulged with illustrations and photographs of slot cars, tool chests, science kits, phonographs, and microscopes, with the shrinking roster of O gauge and HO scale trains crammed into fewer and fewer pages.

The quality of Lionel's promotional artwork declined in the 1960s, as the advertising budget was slashed and staff members departed. Still, the underlying goal remained the same. Since Joshua Cowen had built his first electrical novelties in the opening years of the 20th century, illustrations had helped consumers see what was new and fascinating. Words always tagged along in catalogs and advertisements, but pictures grabbed the attention of youngsters and adults. Illustrators and photographers relied on a range of styles and emphasized different themes to celebrate novel products.

For artists, the challenge had always been finding ways, after observing the latest models, to inject them with life. If successful, their work would have viewers all but swearing that they could hear motors humming and bells ringing or even smell smoke drifting behind steamers. Similarly, illustrators might prove to consumers that new models could somehow improve their lives. Either way, the creators of Lionel art sought to do more than just visually describe the latest offerings. They aimed to convey the wonder, appeal, and magic of electric trains.

Artists had engaged in a symbiotic relationship with the designers of Lionel trains and

LIONEL
1963

"027" Super "O" HO Trains
Standard & HO Motor Racing

The Leader in Model Railroading...The Pioneer in Model Racing

the people using them. Engineers had bequeathed marvelous toys to illustrators, who had transformed cars, locomotives, and accessories into instruments of play and education. Outfits became, in catalog and advertising art, tools by which boys were shaped, fathers

text continues on page 118

The exhilarating cover of the 1963 catalog celebrated Lionel's entry into the field of slot cars, one of the hottest fads for kids in the early 1960s.

By the time Lionel sent stockholders its annual report for 1959, it was pursuing a program of diversification. New owner Roy Cohn wanted to break into the "military-industrial complex." He acquired ownership of a few aerospace firms while continuing to wring money out of the train line. Soon, however, he sold the Airex fishing subsidiary.

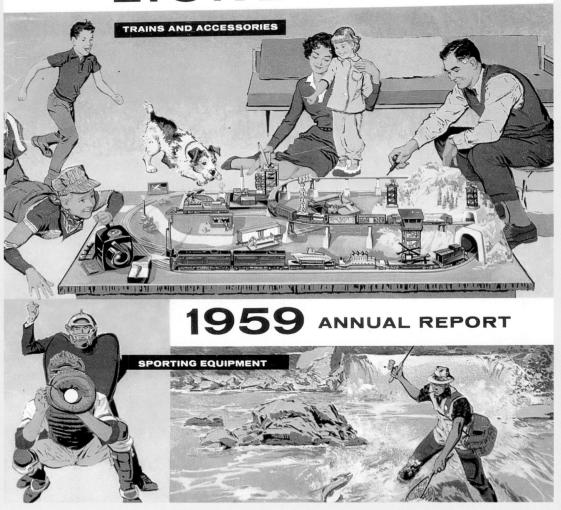

more than trains

Lionel has occasionally tried to diversify its line. It marketed chemistry sets in the 1940s and then challenged Gilbert with its own type of construction toys. Neither effort proved financially successful. Lionel also sought to expand beyond the toy field when it bought the Airex brand of fishing gear in 1947 and later developed a stereoscopic camera sold under the Linex name. Contracts to make items for the military continued after World War II, and Roy Cohn expanded this program between 1959 and 1962 by purchasing small firms in the aerospace industry.

Above: Too bad for Lionel that not every boy was as enamored of the firm's Chem-Lab outfits as the one shown on the cover of this booklet. Written in the form of a comic book, it outlined all the experiments young chemists could perform with the powders and liquids packed in each set. Corinne Synhorst, who wrote this manual during a stint in the advertising department at Lionel, today serves as publisher of the *Saturday Evening Post*.

Left: Kids were no more excited about Lionel's line of construction sets, which was an attempt to challenge the A.C. Gilbert Co. for supremacy in another sector of the toy market. Lionel had deleted the chemistry and construction sets from its line by 1950.

Libby's brings you a lot of train ($24⁹⁵ VALUE) for only $10⁹⁵

To revive sales of its train line, Lionel developed premiums and promotional sets for boys and girls, including this one for Libby's foods. This ad appeared in the October 1963 *Sunset* magazine.

The interdependence of artists, consumers, and designers experienced difficulties, yet managed to survive until the mid-1960s. Then Cohn and his successors, desperate to cut costs because sales were slipping, shredded the mutually reinforcing links by shutting down the Lionel engineering department. As a consequence, no truly new O or O-27 gauge trains joined the line for a number of years, for without engineers how could Lionel innovate? Just the opposite happened. Top executives, feeling less pressure from consumers, opted for the easy course and turned their gaze back to headier times. The trains shown in the catalogs and advertisements, indeed the very images used in those sources, reflected the narrow visions guiding the men in charge.

Lionel brought back older models rather than developing versions of the huge road diesels cruising off assembly lines at General Motors and General Electric. It continued to stock longtime favorites, adorning familiar pieces of rolling stock with unusual paint schemes and railroad heralds. Big accessories disappeared, leaving only signals and gatemen to keep children occupied. Of course, those kids, enchanted by the Gemini astronauts, merely yawned when

rescued, and families strengthened. Consumers, persuaded by what they felt from seeing these images, responded by purchasing the new models and requesting even better ones. Designers gave them what they asked for: trains that neatly balanced elements of whimsy and realism, of color and action. Lionel models became miniature works of beauty and motion. Their look inspired illustrators, whose work contributed to the popularity of these trains.

handed an electric train. Their disappointment and boredom with the Lionel line sent sales plummeting further.

Illustrations of trains suffered, too, as the firm crept back into the past. A picture from the 1950s was recycled for the front of the catalog for 1964, and antique images were plastered across the cover a year later. Outfits and locomotives received short shrift when catalogs swelled in size to accommodate the dozens of science kits and racing cars Lionel was peddling. The preponderance of small black-and-white drawings robbed trains of their magic.

In the late 1960s, when executives pared down the line to prove that Lionel was strictly a toy maker, they forgot that even playthings must be depicted imaginatively to win over children. Instead, trains seemed flat and lifeless, thanks in part to the mediocre pictures used. Images lost so much clarity that readers could not discern the numbers and words stamped on individual cars. Even switching to color photographs to show off the handful of sets available didn't work. Arranging trains on track next to artificial

grass robbed them of the majesty and speed that illustrations had conveyed a decade before. For the powers-that-be to claim that Lionel was a toy conglomerate one year and "The Leader in Model Railroading" the next only revealed how unsure they were.

answers elsewhere

After Roy Cohn lost interest in Lionel, new leaders kept stepping forward with their own schemes for resuscitating Joshua Cowen's grand

The cover of the 1969 catalog milked nostalgia as much as possible. The colors, typeface, and composition recall the 1940 catalog. The speeding locomotives hearken back to the 1950s.

Images of Americana blended with trains in "A Lifetime of Railroading," a poster that Lionel added to its 1970 catalog. The aim was to persuade consumers that they could spend their whole lives playing with toy trains.

O and HO trains to General Mills. Beginning in 1970 and continuing for the next 15 years, divisions of this food giant handled production, which they moved from New Jersey to their own headquarters in Michigan. Like their predecessors, decision-makers in the 1970s and early '80s wracked their brains deciding what to make and how to present their train lines.

With so much tooling already in their hands, the individuals at Model Products Corp. and Fundimensions (the divisions in charge) decided that the smartest and most economical solution was to reissue postwar favorites. Plenty of F3 and Alco diesels and small Hudsons hit the rails pulling familiar gondolas, flatcars, boxcars, and cabooses. To their credit, though, executives realized that new items were also needed. They introduced additional rolling stock and up-to-date engines. Under the hood, however, those locomotives scarcely differed from ones that had been assembled back in the 1950s. Lionel still hesitated to look ahead and take some risks.

This conservative attitude, which steeped Lionel in nostalgia during the years that General Mills supervised train production and sales, influenced the illustrations of the era. The

enterprise. But their actions, as seen in the trains Lionel marketed and the artwork used, revealed their shortcomings and limited visions. Still struggling to define the firm's place in the toy and hobby markets, executives decided in 1969 to lease the rights to manufacture and market the

main function of artwork, corporate leaders believed, was to show what was for sale accurately and economically. Photography was, therefore, the right medium, and artistic renderings all but vanished. Catalogs—who could call them wish books anymore?—resembled brochures for hardware or furniture. Endless color shots of individual items sitting on sections of track or floating against solid backgrounds became the rule. Trains seldom appeared in urban or rural scenes, although such poses, like close-ups and upward angles, would have made models look better.

Advertising directors didn't rid catalog images of all emotional appeal in the 1970s and early '80s. They understood that catalogs still had to capture the imagination of viewers. By and large, however, that meant returning to sentimental, trusted themes and not breaking new ground. Tradition served as their touchstone. Designers selected old-fashioned typefaces and appended vintage catalog images to current ads and posters. When including people in photographs, they rarely used youngsters by themselves. They added male models that viewers would presume were a boy's father or grandfather in order to make the

point that Lionel trains were a family tradition.

Executives found it safer and cheaper during the General Mills years to escape to the past. Mindful of how every dollar was spent, they thought original illustrations, like new tooling and electronics for models of the latest

text continues on page 124

Steam locomotives and logging operations, elements of the past, received top billing on the cover of "Workin' on the Railroad," a manual from 1978.

121

grandpa loves Lionel

Nostalgia—reminding families of how much fun they had enjoyed with their train set years ago—that was the way to rekindle interest in Lionel. At least that's what the executives at General Mills in charge of the line in the 1970s and '80s assumed. With shots of fathers playing on the floor and grandpas smiling benevolently, they hoped to appeal, not so much to kids growing up in this time of Pong and smiley faces, but to their middle-aged fathers. Those aging baby boomers would recall building layouts with their dads and dream of re-creating that same bonding experience with their children.

Above: The cover of the 1973 catalog expands on the familiar theme of a train bringing a boy close to his father. By adding a grandfather, this shot reassures Dad—a child of the postwar era now grown up—that he will benefit most from a Lionel train set.

Right: Not until the 1920s did Lionel remind boys that their fathers likely played with its trains when they were young. Two more decades went by until—with this ad painted by Wesley Neff for the November 30, 1946, *Collier's*—Lionel suggested that grandfathers also knew at first-hand the pleasures and thrills of a model train set.

THE LIONEL CORPORATION
ANNUAL REPORT
YEAR ENDED FEBRUARY 28, 1951

Appealing to three generations occurred very infrequently in postwar artwork. This illustration, done by Raymond Crowley for the 1951 Lionel annual report, jokes about Grandpa taking over the controls rather than trying to make men yearn for a happier time in the past. Here, the dejected grandson waits to take over the transformer.

Everything about this heartwarming illustration by R.J. Tyrrell for the cover of the 1980 catalog screamed nostalgia. Every element—the 19th-century trains, Old West typeface, and quilt on the bed—was intended to hearken back to a simpler, happier time many decades ago.

to reaching Cub Scouts and Little Leaguers, and stockholders would have been ecstatic had there been a revival of interest among kids. But the "boys" most likely to respond to the trains and art tended to be quite a bit older.

rekindling the interest

Something amazing happened to the toy train hobby during the 1970s and '80s. At a time when most kids could not be bothered with what Lionel was offering, another group was discovering to its delight that the company was still in business. They were baby boomers who had owned sets in the 1950s. Now grown up, with children of their own not to mention plenty of discretionary income, they remembered their Santa Fe F3s, automatic milk cars, and log loaders. General Mills looked to dads to rekindle enthusiasm for Lionel. No wonder they published photographs showing casually dressed fathers and grandfathers joining kids in playing with O gauge sets. The postwar dream of security had returned to gladden men. Yearning for an imaginary past, they bought trains in hopes of imparting that sense of reassurance to their offspring.

locomotives, were luxuries they could do without. As a result, Lionel catalogs looked the same from one year to the next. Gone were the days when each had its own flavor and unique art gave it personality. Function and not form was uppermost, as designers hoped that nostalgic images would revive sales. They paid lip service

Artwork, deprived of new and distinctive models to glamorize, struggled to convey feelings of nostalgia. Once illustrations had expressed the belief that operating Lionel trains taught boys how to shape their destiny and master the future. In the 1970s and '80s, however, the underlying message changed. Art and photographs increasingly promised those grown-up boys that returning to an innocent past was possible . . . and worthwhile.

The fears associated with becoming an adult had proved all too real. Illustrations in the 1950s had warned that joining the rat race wore down a man's spunk and hope. Back then, his son might bring back his smile by inviting him to play with a Lionel outfit. Decades later, this paternal bargain had been turned upside down. The boys of the '50s had grown up and become the young Turks who were now finding that life in the fast lane offered few genuine satisfactions. But these frustrated fathers couldn't turn to their children to save them because current playthings seemed alien and complicated to them. Middle-aged baby boomers could not identify with the video games and light sabers their sons cherished. The solution, according to catalog photographs, was for men to buy new sets and rediscover the happiness of operating trains and building layouts.

The dreams of nostalgia promoted by General Mills had only one flaw. The new trains may have looked like their postwar ancestors, but they didn't feel or sound or smell like the ones baby boomers recalled. So men ignored them and hunted for the sets they had received and the accessories they had wished

text continues on page 128

Not a real kid in sight in this humorous ad, which appeared in the November 1981 issue of *Ambassador,* the magazine Trans-World Airlines provided passengers. Lionel acknowledged that it directed its top-of-the-line trains at the baby boomers that had loved its trains as youngsters.

**Fun for all with these Exciting
LIONEL TRAINS**

Above: This ad from the November 1949
Mechanix Illustrated leaves no doubt that the
boy of the family still claimed the Lionel set.
Families pinned their hopes for the future on
him; mothers and sisters were expected to offer
the support he needed to have fun and grow.

Right: Why should little Joe or Terry have all the
fun? Beginning in the 1930s, Lionel encouraged—sometimes nagged—fathers to join their
sons in constructing model railroads. Both
would benefit, as seen in this Sunday comic
from the *Detroit News* of December 6, 1936.

the dreams of families

Once insistent that electric trains were strictly for boys, Lionel has, over
the past half-century, helped transform model railroading into an activity for the entire family. During the final decade of the pre-World War
II era, art portrayed fathers joining their sons in building layouts. After
the war, illustrations and photographs included mothers and daughters
to suggest that families felt more secure when they engaged in a pastime together. Lionel returned to this theme in the 1970s and '80s, but
centered on Dad, the grown-up boy of the postwar era.

LIONEL® 027

1974

Perhaps the freckle-faced kid pictured in 1949 matured into the devoted dad shown on the cover of the 1974 catalog. Weighed down by many responsibilities, he needed time to unwind and discover the joys of fatherhood. A Lionel train set provided the answer. This time, however, his daughters are the ones nurturing his love affair with toy trains.

COLLECTOR SERIES, 1982

once played with or dreamed of owning scarcely cared about the costs. They insisted on finding the trains of their youth and gladly handed over wads of cash for a locomotive or passenger set or original catalog that might fulfill their urge to recapture the joy and innocence of boyhood. Nostalgia drove them, but not the artificial kind cultivated by Lionel advertising. Collectors had little use for the current line because it failed to meet their emotional needs. The trains made by General Mills didn't make them feel secure and young again.

new sources of art

Photographs and illustrations in catalogs never relented in the campaign to link new Lionel models with the nostalgic yearnings of grown baby boomers. They showed boys enjoying electric trains in the company of fathers and sometimes mothers or grandparents to inspire men to buy new sets for their sons or themselves. The images no longer suggested that a boy would not be able to function as an adult if he never received a train. Instead, they emphasized that dads and their kids deserved the pleasures only a Lionel outfit could bring. Why should they miss out by not owning one?

The images Lionel created in the 1970s and

General Mills developed some models of contemporary locomotives and updated many postwar favorites during the years it produced the Lionel line. Nevertheless, the five beauties on the cover of the 1982 catalog failed to satisfy collectors whose hearts languished in the 1950s.

for long ago. They attended swap meets and mailed "want lists" to dealers specializing in vintage trains. Demand for postwar as well as prewar trains exploded, which caused prices for models in excellent and like new condition to shoot upward.

So what? Guys eager to acquire what they had

'80s reflected changing views of manhood in America. Once, prevailing notions emphasized productivity and authority, especially in a father's relationship with his son. By the late 20th century, though, being a man touched on enjoying life and fitting in with those who were younger and supposedly more attuned to the latest fashions and values. Men needed Lionel trains as much or even more than their sons did so that they could remain young at heart and not grow apart from their sons or lose their memories of their fathers.

Electric trains remained essential to feeling successful and happy, or so Lionel advertising continued to claim. Joshua Cowen would have nodded in approval if he could have seen how the trains he had developed went on fulfilling the hopes of his "boys." But he would have been disappointed to realize that Lionel artwork wasn't sparking the current interest. Photographs merely showed what was being produced in the 1980s, and the few paintings published in the catalogs were better at portraying evocative rail scenes than recapturing the splendor and thrills of O gauge modeling in the postwar period.

Memories—mental images—were responsible for the sweeping toy train fever. What aging

baby boomers remembered of ripping open gift-wrapped Lionel outfits, building layouts with their fathers, and hoarding nickels and dimes until they had enough cash to buy another signal or boxcar fueled their passion. Vintage illustrations nourished their recollections, and

Learning from L. Meinrad Mayer and Robert Sherman, the artist that did the cover of the 1983 catalog depicted only the front of a new Southern Pacific steamer. The lights, smoke, steam, and color stand out.

TRAIN SETS

YARD CHIEF

For those of you who want a high quality Lionel train and prefer to build your own customized layout, this beautifully designed New York Central work train is first class from locomotive to caboose.

Photographs of the actual trains appeared with a fanciful illustration of the Yard Chief outfit inching away from the skyline of Manhattan in the 1984 catalog. The set looks great, although it's riding on two-rail track.

collectors avidly sought original catalogs and advertisements; new images, however well-staged and carefully photographed, too often left them hungry.

When artwork did catch up with the revival of interest in the 1990s, it came from a different quarter. Illustrators familiar with the toy train hobby painted scenes that beautifully expressed

the nostalgia felt by middle-aged collectors. Angela Trotta Thomas, introduced to the hobby by her husband, led the way. On prints, greeting cards, and magazine covers, she painted the scenes that baby boomers reminisce about. Her illustrations showed boys admiring Lionel displays in store windows of the 1950s or unpacking set boxes on Christmas morning. Thomas created a world of make-believe in which every lad received the outfit he dreamed of and discovered that his dad couldn't wait to help him assemble the track and get the train going.

Warm, romantic illustrations of boys and their trains retained their popularity through the 1990s. Other amateur artists, seeing the financial rewards that Thomas was reaping, followed her lead. Lionel didn't abandon the "nostalgia sweepstakes" either, to judge by the trains and artwork found in its catalogs. All the same, Richard Kughn, the real estate developer and toy train enthusiast who acquired control of the line in 1985, recognized the limitations of focusing on the past. Eager to revive the fortunes of Lionel and restore its reputation for innovation, he insisted on looking ahead. Products and illustrations reflected his vision and ushered in yet another era of achievement there.

In paintings such as "High Hopes" (first shown in the December 1996 *Classic Toy Trains* magazine), Angela Trotta Thomas revived memories of playing with Lionel trains for countless middle-aged baby boomers. Blending accurate pictures of vintage trains with nostalgic scenes has earned her acclaim among collectors.

chapter six

Dreams of tomorrow
1990-2003

For almost two decades, beginning not long after Richard Kughn bought the assets of the company in 1985, Lionel has directed its attention to the future. The dominant dreams now, shared by executives and consumers, relate to constant improvement in the technical aspects of its toy trains and art. Under the leadership of Kughn, followed by Gary Moreau, Richard Maddox, and now William Bracy, Lionel has sought to make more realistic, better-performing locomotives and rolling stock by capitalizing on breakthroughs in the development of can-style motors, light-emitting diodes, computer chips, and tiny audio components. The results are nothing short of astounding.

The trains and accessories currently available surpass in virtually every respect anything that Lionel produced before. Technology promises more improvements in the future, including in the photography and computer graphics used in advertising. Little wonder that Lionel executives look ahead with optimism.

But feeling hopeful about the future and embracing technological innovations as the key to ongoing growth have not diminished the importance of nostalgia. Decision-makers involved with sales and engineering continue to keep one eye on the past. They would be foolish to do anything else because so many Lionel customers complain whenever they suspect the firm is moving ahead too fast and betraying its heritage.

new masters

Executives at Lionel walk a tightrope as they strive to meet the expectations of middle-aged baby boomers. On the one hand, they want to develop an outstanding line of up-to-date mod-

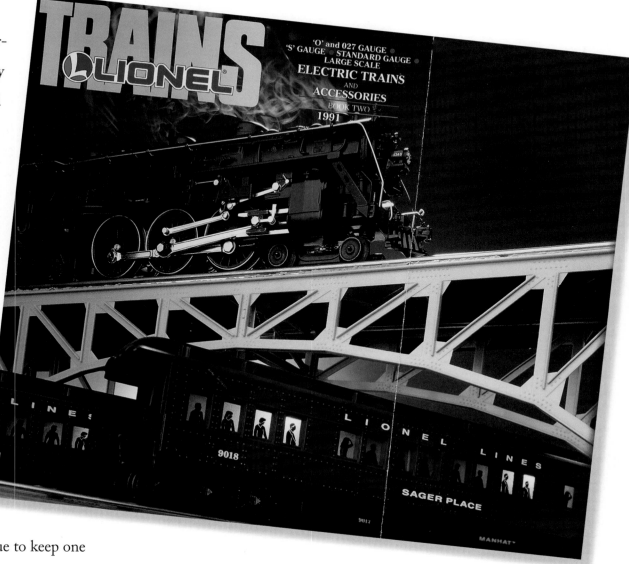

els that will lead the company into the future. On the other hand, decision-makers know they must respect Lionel's traditions and feed the nostalgia that motivates numbers of the men who buy its trains. The quest for a balanced line continues to shape and be shaped by Lionel artwork. More exactly, illustrations help persuade consumers that ties to the past remain strong.

Fritz Von Tagen shot this cover for the 1991 catalog just as he would have photographed full-sized trains. The result is a dramatic, realistic scene that makes the trains look great.

Champions
that refuse to die.

Computer-generated graphics let Lionel inject its illustrations with spark that complements the improvements made in the electronics and appearance of new models. You can almost feel the trains in this ad from the July 1996 issue of *Classic Toy Trains* fly by in the early morning.

Art used in recent Lionel catalogs and advertising reflects the challenge facing corporate leaders. Obviously, the masters responsible for various illustrations and photographs imitate others at Lionel by seizing on new technology and discovering its benefits. They use computer graphics and programs, along with state-of-the-art camera equipment, to create superb images that, like earlier ones, aim to make the new trains and accessories look exciting and accurate.

Consider how Fritz Von Tagen transformed the covers of Lionel catalogs in the late 1980s and early '90s with photographs that dramatically posed trains against black backgrounds. He experimented with lighting and special effects involving smoke and shadow to create a

sophisticated look for the catalogs at a time when Kughn wanted to break away from the nostalgia that seemed to be holding back Lionel. More recently, artists using conventional and computer-generated images have concentrated on the innovative aspects of new trains. Steve Davis, for one, exaggerates some of the details and colors on items in hopes of nurturing impressions of size and speed. Backdrops remain important in framing scenes that enhance the realism of trains. Although the images filling new catalogs and advertisements certainly look different from previous illustrations, the techniques and tricks artists use merely build on what L. Meinrad Mayer pioneered in the 1930s and Robert Sherman refined a decade and more later.

Artists dare not, however, forget about nostalgia. Like the executives planning what's developed, they have to find ways of integrating the past into the present. That means using venerated styles and compositions to strengthen the spell that Lionel casts over its customers. Illustrators thus find themselves in the somewhat ironic position that designers know only too well: utilizing the latest tools, they re-create elements of a bygone era. Catalogs feature scenes that hearken back to earlier times and even use well-known motifs from past wish books. Magazine advertising in the 1990s posed brand-new trains and novel accessories with items and human models to bring back memories of images developed during the postwar and sometimes the prewar periods. The message underlying recent Lionel art is plain: Our new trains have never been more mechanically advanced, but you'll find them as comforting as ever.

Lionel does not force this message into most of its artwork. To do so would frustrate customers and create the impression that it was unable or unwilling to change with the times. Instead, the vast majority of illustrations in new catalogs amount to simple color photographs of individual items. Art directors pose trains amid model railroad scenery or on solid backgrounds to help potential buyers make informed decisions about what to purchase. People, whether children or adults, appear with trains only infrequently because Lionel aims to sell trains in a segmented market rather than

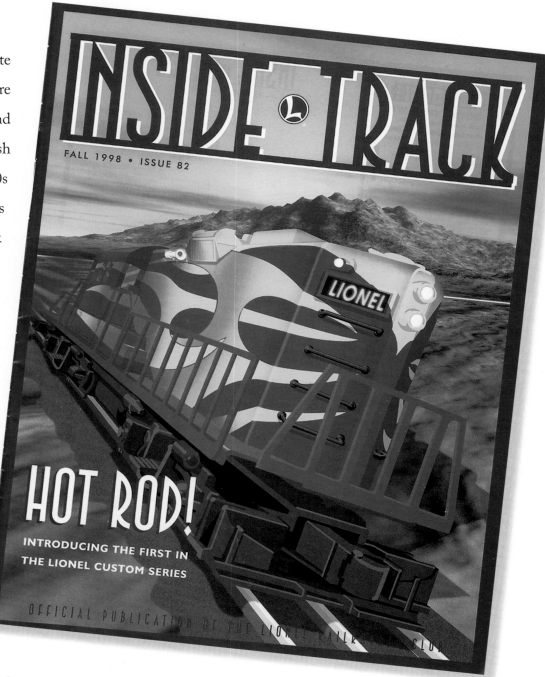

provide security or lead the entire industry. In this sense, recent artwork takes the limited approach characteristic of the time when General Mills produced the Lionel line. The company's grandiose aims of the Roaring

text continues on page 138

Computers have opened a new world for artists like Steve Davis. His souped-up road diesel screams toward us, ready to bound off the cover of the Fall 1998 issue of *Inside Track*.

135

Going somewhere fast?

2380

LIONEL
MAGNE-TRACTION

Fly Magne-Traction.

When you need to get somewhere fast, there's only one train with the curve-gripping security of Magne-Traction. More speed, more power, more pull. Exclusively from Lionel.

LIONEL

© 1996 Lionel LLC. All material contained herein is the property of Lionel LLC. Lionel and Magne-Traction are registered trademarks and 2380 is a trademark of Lionel LLC.

Above: Kids love to race locomotives and give their trains steep grades to climb, so engineers used advances in powder metallurgy and electromagnets to develop Magne-Traction in 1949. Decades later, well into the computer age, Lionel hyped it again, as seen in this ad from the July 1996 issue of *Classic Toy Trains* magazine.

Right: Command control, sound system, fan-driven smoke unit, speed control, and directional lighting don't exhaust the list of features on current top-of-the-line locomotives, such as this SD80MAC, shown in a computer-generated illustration from the 2002 catalog.

into the future

Enjoyable, instructive, colorful, fast—these adjectives have fit Lionel trains for most of the past century. Designers and engineers continue to improve their design and operation by capitalizing on changes in manufacturing, especially in the field of electronics, so Lionel trains can run flawlessly. Lionel has also linked its miniature trains with social and technological breakthroughs. What streamlining was to the 1930s, space exploration became to the 1950s and '60s. Today, of course, computers fascinate, and Lionel has used them both to equip its locomotives with superior sound effects and control systems and to generate accurate images of those models in recent catalogs.

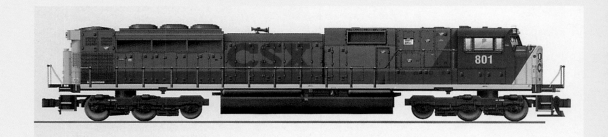

LIONEL

"027"   SUPER "O"   HO

Technology of a different sort—linked with firing missiles into space and exploring distant planets—fascinated Americans in the late 1950s and '60s. Lionel responded, as the cover of the 1958 catalog reveals, with accessories that launched rockets and freight cars that hauled satellites.

This ad in the June 1992 *Classic Toy Trains* announced a new accessory with a model dressed like an engineer. It also showed him in the cab of a postwar steamer in a pose reminiscent of the cover of the 1925 catalog.

Twenties and Fabulous Fifties, like the sumptuous art from those years, have vanished.

Even so, just as each new catalog features a plethora of steam locomotives and reissues of prewar and postwar favorites, so do nostalgic images continue to appear in Lionel artwork.

Angela Trotta Thomas has been commissioned to execute catalog covers and brochures. Illustrators use a host of vintage scenes, including many that touch on the company's history, to promote recent offerings. Artists, along with Lionel's engineers and sales force, understand that consumers need gentle yet constant reminders that this is still the company they loved when they were youngsters.

dreams ahead

Where does this leave things? Once more, Lionel attempts, with its trains and its art, to satisfy different markets, including consumers with conflicting desires. For certain enthusiasts, especially younger ones who feel comfortable with computers and enjoy video games, Lionel highlights cutting-edge technology. Illustrations use new tools and media and reinforce the notion that Lionel is pushing forward to bring out trains that surpass anything ever developed before. Their goal is to refurbish the image of Lionel, particularly when competition has intensified over the past 10 to 15 years, and guarantee that people will not consider its trains to be mere relics.

At the same time that Lionel is shifting its gaze to the future and heralding technological advances, it feels compelled to reach out to older consumers, whose loyalty remains intense. These hobbyists have supported the company for many years and remain the primary market for the massive locomotives and intricate accessories at the top of the line. Art plays a critical role in this process, since it can lead the way in depicting new trains as elements in a great tradition rather than departures from it.

Maintaining a balance between futuristic technology and nostalgic yearnings remains as significant a challenge for management in the early 21st century as blending realism and whimsy was for executives in the middle of the 20th. Once the answer was to catalog a scale Hudson at one end of the line and lithographed O-27 sets at the other. Today the solution is to fill the top end with state-of-the-art die-cast models running on computer chips and offer starter sets using conventional methods of control at the low end. Even individual items reflect the search for an ideal medium, with models of vintage locomotives boasting the latest in command control and sound effects.

The components of the line may have changed, but the underlying philosophy has survived since the 1920s, when Lionel marketed both Standard and O gauge trains to expand its customer base. And that has meant that the central place of art remains to show how innovation and change are still linked with familiar forms and messages. So consumers have never stopped believing that their trains can enhance their lives while keeping them entertained.

text continues on page 142

Art has returned to the theme of realistic paint schemes and sophisticated electronics on models of the latest locomotives. There's nothing wrong with this perspective, except that in this ad from the May 1994 *Classic Toy Trains* magazine Lionel seems to have forgotten that its trains run on three rails.

**Words can't say
what a Lionel can.**

Once upon a time, Christmas came frosted with
the magical wonder only a child can feel. One
of the most magical things about it was your
Lionel train.
And your Dad was there. Showing you how to
lay the track. Connect the wires. Work the
transformer so the train moved backwards and forwards, fast and slow.
You didn't know it at the time, and he never said it. But that
Lionel train was his way of keeping you
close a little bit longer, of making sure

you knew he cared.
In 90 years, that hasn't changed. When parents give a Lionel
to their own child, it can bring all those feelings back as if they
were happening for the very first time.
This Christmas, put a Lionel train on your shopping list. Call
us at 1-800-90-TRAIN, and we'll tell you where to find a complete selection of Lionel trains near you.
Because the most precious gift is a lasting memory. And that's
something that just can't be put
into words.

LIONEL
Because no childhood should be without a train.

Above: Artists started promoting the link
between Lionel trains and Christmas in the
1920s. This theme has never departed from
the company's advertising, and it occasionally
influences ads run by other firms. Among
recent depictions is this photograph from the
December 1990 *Life*.

Right: Decades earlier, the new O gauge
model of the *Hiawatha* was shown bursting
forth in an illustration C. Weimer did for the
cover of the November-December 1935
Lionel Magazine.

always at Christmas

Having an electric train endlessly run around a Christmas tree has become a tradition in countless households in America. No one knows for sure when and where this practice began. What is certain is that for many families it has become as much a part of the holiday celebration as gaily wrapped gifts stacked under the tree and a festive meal. Lionel has capitalized on the public's association of its trains with Christmas, and artists used their talents to create memorable images.

Left: The postwar decades were magical times when kids opened packages containing Lionel sets. The joy of discovering a layout built under the tree comes forth in an illustration done by Philip Huestis (a member of the Lionel advertising department) for the December 1947 *Model Builder*.

Below: So universal was the connection between a happy, secure childhood and owning a Lionel train that various businesses used it in their advertising. James Crabb captured every boy's dream in a painting used to advertise products made by Weirton Steel Co. in the December 1952 *Better Homes & Gardens*.

The decades slip away as you look at the cover of a brochure Lionel created to promote its Century Club entries in 1997. The skyscrapers and propeller-driven plane suggest Gotham in the 1930s, while the pose of the locomotives brings back memories of the 1938 catalog.

The underlying meaning of Lionel art has scarcely changed because at the most basic level the most important dream associated with toy trains has remained the same. Children and adults long to duplicate a slice of real life at home. The power of this urge hasn't diminished in the century since Joshua Cohen demonstrated his first train. Whether that train operates through a simple transformer or a handheld computer, we cherish the opportunity to make it move on command. And we equally cherish the belief expressed in diverse images that our trains can make us happier and better. So long as we trust that Lionel trains can fulfill our dreams, its artwork will touch our hearts and guide us into a land of magic.

Left: Four superb postwar locomotives returned to the line, each equipped with state-of-the-art features, such as TrainMaster Command Control, Railsounds, Towercom, and Crewtalk. This ad from the January 1999 *Classic Toy Trains* rekindles memories of the 1950s.

Below: Sometimes the simplest images are the most powerful. The Erie 4-6-2 Pacific fills the entire spread in this ad from the July 2001 *Classic Toy Trains*. The crisp details of this locomotive, especially the beam of its headlight, contrast with the indistinct backdrop.